Burglars on the Job

Advisor in Criminal Justice to Northeastern University Press
Gilbert Geis

Burglars on the Job

Streetlife and Residential Break-ins

Richard T. Wright
Scott H. Decker

NORTHEASTERN UNIVERSITY PRESS / BOSTON
Published by University Press of New England
Hanover and London

NORTHEASTERN UNIVERSITY PRESS
Published by University Press of New England
One Court Street, Lebanon, NH 03766
www.upne.com

Printed in the United States of America   10   9   8

ISBN-13: 978-1-55553-271-0
ISBN-10: 1-55553-271-3

Library of Congress Cataloging-in-Publication Data

Wright, Richard.
    Burglars on the job : streetlife and residential break-ins /
Richard T. Wright, Scott Decker.
        p.   cm.
    Includes bibliographical references and index.
    ISBN 1 — 55553 — 185 — 7 (alk. paper);
    ISBN 1 — 55553 — 271 — 3 (pbk.: alk. paper)
    1. Burglary — Missouri — Saint Louis.   2. Burglars —
Missouri — Saint Louis.   I. Decker, Scott.   II. Title.
HV6661.M8W75   1994
364.1'62 — dc20   93-44357

To Gil Geis, the Babe Ruth of criminology

Keep hittin' 'em out of the park!

Contents

THERE ARE SOME extraordinarily compelling vignettes in this excellent field study of burglars by Richard Wright and Scott Decker. One that particularly caught my fancy was the rapture of some burglars when they found themselves surrounded by all those wonderful things in the house they had illegally entered. Everything—anything—is theirs for the taking, presuming they can carry it away without being observed and taken captive. One is reminded of the ecstasy conveyed by Charlie Chaplin in one of his antic movies when he finds himself locked in a large well-stocked department store overnight.

There are other insights in this detailed study that epitomize essential ingredients of the crime of burglary as it is experienced by those who commit it. There is the ominous fear, expressed by many of the offenders, that when they enter a dwelling its occupant will be waiting for them, right there, with a shotgun that will blast their heads into pieces. And there is the tension between grabbing what is readily available and getting out of there quickly, or lingering a bit longer to pick up other goodies, but thereby increasing by some unknown but frightening fraction the possibility of being discovered.

Most essentially, there is the strong focus in this field study on the pressures, internal and external, that drive human beings to break into the living quarters of other human beings and take whatever there is of value that they can locate and comfortably carry away. It is these pressures as they bear on particular persons in particular circumstances that for the authors lie at the heart of an understanding of the dynamics of the criminal offense of burglary.

Ideas and information were gathered through locating and gaining the cooperation of men and women who had done and were continuing to do burglaries. What most differentiates *Burglars on the Job* from the handful of inquiries that have reached out to the criminal protagonist to seek understanding of the offense of burglary and the person of the burglar is that the sources here are men and women on the streets. They are offenders who are not constrained by incarceration and the concomitant impact that being caught and imprisoned has on retrospective thoughts about the crimes that got them into such difficulty. It is one thing to talk about failure, another to discuss contemporaneously behavior that is succeeding but which at any moment may end disastrously.

Probably more than anyone else, Malcolm X, a burglar before he became so highly respected as a leader in the black civil rights movement, taught the public the relative advantages of burglary. Malcolm expressed in his autobiography (*The Autobiography of Malcolm X* [New York: Grove Press, 1965]) many of the same feelings and attitudes that Wright and Decker encountered when they went out into the streets of St. Louis to talk with their informants:

> I had learned from the pros, and from my own experience, how important it was to be careful and plan. Burglary, properly executed, though it had its dangers, offered the maximum chances of success with the minimum risk. If you did your job so that you never met any of your victims, it lessened your chances of having to attack or perhaps kill someone. And if through some slip-up you were caught, later, by the police, there was never a positive eyewitness (1965:141–42).

Throughout *Burglars on the Job*, its authors alter our ideas about crime and, in particular, about the offense of burglary on the basis of what they learned from those who work at it. They note, for instance, that many highly heralded protective devices often do not discourage burglars because they already are committed to the deed by the time they discover the existence of such barriers. On the other hand, there is considerable evidence that some shields, most notably large and noisy dogs, can readily convince many to go elsewhere to practice their trade. There also is the paradoxical finding that certain kinds of safeguards used by homeowners sometimes only encourage burglary by communicating to the offender the idea that there are expensive things within the dwelling.

This book is a particularly significant contribution to a school of thought in criminology that finds demographic and other fashionably current explanations of offending inadequate and asks instead that attention be accorded to the immediate considerations that produce an offense. Jack Katz highlighted this view in his pathbreaking monograph *Seductions of Crime: Moral and Sensual Attractions in Doing Evil* (New York: Basic Books, 1988). How do you explain, Katz asked rhetorically, an offender who on many days walks past a jewelry store with barely a notice, but on one particular day decides to break the window and help himself to some of the merchandise. After all, his age, his psychological complexes, and his relationship to his peers and parents (as well as those various other characteristics considered by mainline criminologists to be explanatory) were no different on the earlier days than they were when the offense was carried out. Background factors may tell us in a general and statistical sense who might at some time commit a crime, but they do not tell us why a particular crime was committed when it was by a particular person.

It is this kind of focus that pervades *Burglars on the Job*. In a noteworthy concluding chapter, the authors set forth their theoretical stance, and tell us what they have learned by dealing with burglars, as they denote it, "in the wild." They point out the difficulties and dangers of an approach such as theirs. The careful reader will come to appreciate from this material—and from other hints here and there throughout the volume—the enormity of the research enterprise, and why so few studies of this kind are carried out, however basic and intellectually valuable they may be.

Criminological research today has a considerable tendency to rely on large data sets from which findings emerge which, at best, are merely mildly interesting. Presently research with a direct policy relevance is in fashion, particularly inquiries which test this or that rearrangement of law enforcement procedures or criminal justice agency practices. The truth is that no criminal justice tinkering—be it with such matters as the nature of police patrols, the death penalty, or sentencing guidelines—is going to have more than the merest marginal impact on the extent of crime in this country, if it has any impact at all. It seems to me that we must begin to understand how people who commit offenses view their behavior and how such views can be influenced before we will see any notable change in crime levels. Admittedly this is a gigantic task, but I would insist that the kind of tough and basic work and interpretation that has gone into *Burglars on the Job* represents one of our best paths toward that end.

GILBERT GEIS
UNIVERSITY OF CALIFORNIA, IRVINE

Acknowledgments

THROUGHOUT THE CONDUCT of the study on which this book is based, we received help and advice from many people. Howard Becker guided us through a maze of qualitative data software packages, pointing out the relative advantages and disadvantages of each for the kind of work we had in mind. In introducing us to "GOFER," he made a match that seems likely to last a lifetime. George McCall participated in the development of our interview and observational research instruments and assisted us in pretesting these materials. R. Gil Kerlikowske, Carl Klockars, and Al Reiss oversaw the entire data collection process, even going so far as to venture into the field with us one night in near-blizzard conditions. Allison Redfern (now Rooney) and Laurie Mitchell undertook the daunting task of managing the day-to-day administrative and organizational duties inherent in a project of this magnitude. Dietrich Smith, a.k.a. "Street Daddy," was by our side every step of the way. For keeping us safe, we owe him a special debt of gratitude.

As anyone who has carried out field-based research knows, the real work begins when it comes time to write up the results. Here too we were fortunate in being able to fall back on the counsel of wise and patient friends. Gil Geis and Linda Jeffery each read the entire manuscript, making many helpful editorial suggestions along the way. Trevor Bennett and Neal Shover also read and commented on much of what we wrote; both of them kept the pressure on us to draw out the wider implications of our findings for explanations of offender decision making. Others who provided us with encouragement

Acknowledgments

and constructive criticism as the writing progressed include Eric Baumer, JoAnn Decker, Rhonda Dodd, Theo Harman, Dick Hobbs, Terry Jones, Janet Lauritsen, Michael Stein, Rick Rosenfeld, Nigel Walker, and D. J. West.

Portions of this book were drafted during a year-long research leave spent in Cambridge and Durham, two of the most beautiful cities in the United Kingdom. We wish to thank Anthony Bottoms, Director of the Institute of Criminology, Cambridge University, for providing an office and access to one of the world's great criminology libraries during the Michaelmas Term, 1991. We also are grateful to Richard Brown, Head of the Department of Sociology and Social Policy, University of Durham, for his kindness in making available office space for the Epiphany and Lent Terms, 1992. Further, we want to thank James Barber, Master of Hatfield College, Durham, for food, shelter, and the warm hospitality for which the college is renowned.

Our project was funded by Grant No. 89-IJ-CX-0046 from the National Institute of Justice. A happy by-product of this fact was that Winnie Reed acted as our program manager. She was unswervingly supportive and fair-minded throughout the entire course of the research; working with her really was a pleasure. We are required to state that the points of view or opinions expressed in this book are ours and do not necessarily represent the official position or policies of the U.S. Department of Justice. But we hope that they are impressed with our effort.

RICHARD T. WRIGHT
SCOTT H. DECKER

Burglars on the Job

Introduction

THIS IS A BOOK ABOUT the offender's perspective on the
process of committing residential burglaries. It aims to understand such offenses through the eyes of those who commit
them. What leads to residential burglaries? How are they
done? What does it feel like to do them? No one is better
placed to answer such questions than the offender. Yet the
offender's perspective has received only a small amount of attention from criminological researchers (Walker, 1984; Wright
and Bennett, 1990), though it is of crucial importance to the
formulation of both theory and policy. In regard to theory, the
factors often said to be associated with lawbreaking must be
linked to crime through the perceptions and decision-making
processes of offenders. Making this point, Glueck (quoted in
Bovet, 1951:20) has observed: "A factor cannot be a cause before it is a motive." Similarly, Toch (1987:152) has argued that
"Criminology can benefit by illuminating the 'black box' (of-

fender perspectives) that intervenes between conventional independent variables (criminogenic influences) and dependent
variables (antisocial behavior)." And Walker (1984:viii) has
gone so far as to maintain that criminological theorists are
"wasting their time" if they do not consider the mental states
of criminals as they contemplate the commission of offenses.
There is a great debate in criminological circles, for example,
about the extent to which property offenders are "rational" in
their approach to lawbreaking (Hirschi, 1986; Walsh, 1986).
This debate cannot be resolved satisfactorily without a solid
understanding of how such offenders perceive and interpret
their own circumstances and opportunities (Clarke and Cornish, 1985).

Criminal justice policymaking, much of which is based on
assumptions about the perceptions of criminals (Bennett and
Wright, 1984), also requires a firmer understanding of the offender's perspective. The traditional policy of deterrence rests
squarely on the notion that offenders are utilitarian persons,
who carefully weigh the potential costs and rewards of their
illegal actions. Policymakers attempt to increase the perceived
costs of crime (by enhancing the chances that the offender will
be apprehended or will receive a severe penalty) and thereby to
"tip the balance" toward nonoffending. Likewise, situational
crime prevention strategies — such as lock installation and
property-marking campaigns — assume that offenders are influenced by such tactics. They seek to alter matters so that
potential lawbreakers will decide that an offense is too risky,
too unrewarding, or too difficult.

But little is known about how criminals make decisions in
relation to (1) the threat of apprehension and official penalties
(Beyleveld, 1980; Henshel and Carey, 1975; Tunnell, 1992) or
(2) the alteration of situational features (Mayhew, 1979;
Mayhew et al., 1979). Lamenting this state of affairs, Feeney
(1986:68) has noted: "If headway ever is to be made in dealing
with crime, we must access the information that offenders
have." In the absence of this kind of research, there is a danger
of wasting public money on crime prevention projects that

may ultimately reduce the quality of life more than they alter the opportunities for crime.

Reasons for the neglect of the offender's perspective are not difficult to discern. Tapping into that perspective calls for the use of research designs that allow offenders to "speak for themselves." Positivism, which has dominated criminology for decades, traditionally has dismissed such designs as "soft" or "unscientific" (Toch, 1987). What is more, these approaches often require that researchers deal directly with offenders in the field—something that criminologists have been reluctant to do (Chambliss, 1975; Polsky, 1969). Recently, however, positivism has become more amenable to the offender's perspective (Gottfredson and Hirschi, 1987). And researchers, especially those with crime prevention policy concerns, have shown increased interest in lawbreakers' perceptions and decision making (e.g., Feeney, 1986; Tunnell, 1992).

To date, research on the offender's perspective has focussed disproportionately on residential burglary (e.g., Bennett and Wright, 1984; Rengert and Wasilchick, 1985), with most of the work based on interviews with incarcerated offenders. These studies are open to criticism on several grounds. First, criminologists long have suspected that offenders do not behave naturally when they are in criminal justice settings. More than two decades ago, for example, Sutherland and Cressey (1970:68) argued: "Those who have had intimate contacts with criminals 'in the open' know that criminals are not 'natural' in police stations, courts, and prisons, and that they must be studied in their everyday life outside of institutions if they are to be understood." Second, it is clear that the accounts offered by some incarcerated offenders are distorted because they are gathered in the prison environment (e.g., Cromwell et al., 1991). Assurances of confidentiality notwithstanding, many prisoners remain convinced that what they say will affect their chances of being released and, therefore, they portray themselves in the best possible light. Finally, as McCall (1978:27) has cautioned, studies of incarcerated offenders are vulnerable to the charge that they are based on "unsuccessful criminals, on the supposition that successful criminals are not apprehended or at least are able to avoid incarceration." This charge, McCall continues, is "the most central bogeyman in the criminologist's demonology" (see also Hagedorn, 1990; Watters and Biernacki, 1989).

Despite such criticisms, it must be granted that, because most criminologists have shied away from studying criminals "in the wild," there is little hard evidence available on which to judge whether active offenders really do think and act differently than their incarcerated counterparts. The reluctance to study offenders in the field is attributable to a variety of factors. Walker (1984:viii), for instance, has observed that there is "easier game" for criminological researchers to go after: they can reanalyze official data and study the agencies of criminal justice. Probably the most important reason for their reticence, however, is a longstanding belief that this type of research is impractical. In particular, how is one to locate active criminals and obtain their cooperation?

Chambliss has challenged the entrenched notion that field-based studies of active offenders are unworkable, asserting,

> The data on organized crime and professional theft as well
> as other presumably difficult-to-study events are much
> more available than we usually think. All we really have to
> do is to get out of our offices and onto the street. The data
> are there; the problem is that too often [researchers] are not.
> (Chambliss, 1975:39)

Those who have carried out field research with active criminals would no doubt regard this assertion as overly simplistic, but they probably would concur that it is easier to locate such offenders and to gain their confidence than commonly is presumed. As Hagedorn (1990:251) has argued: "Any good field researcher . . . willing to spend the long hours necessary to develop good informants can solve the problem of access." Cromwell et al. (1991) managed to recruit 30 active offenders for their study of residential burglary in Midland, Texas. And Rengert and Wasilchick (1989) contacted 15 free-world offenders for a similar project in Philadelphia. There is a crying need for a larger investigation of this type; among other things, such an investigation could throw substantial light on the extent to which information obtained from residential burglars in their "natural habitat" differs from that provided by comparable offenders in a criminal justice setting.

The Present Study

The study of residential burglary on which this book is based was conducted on the streets of St. Louis, Missouri, a declining "rust belt" city. St. Louis has fallen victim to some of the same problems that have plagued other American cities in the post-World War II era, namely deindustrialization followed by rapid population loss and the concentration of poverty. However, these problems have been writ large in St. Louis owing to its limited size relative to the surrounding metropolitan area; as urban decay took hold, residents with the financial ability to do so—both black and white—moved out of the city and into one of the more desirable communities on its borders, taking much of the tax base with them. Left behind in this process were "the truly disadvantaged" (Wilson, 1987), people with few resources and a consequent need for social services that have become impossible to maintain in the face of decreasing revenues. The crime rate in St. Louis consistently outpaces that for most other cities in the United States; for instance, its 1988 burglary rate, at 2,950 per 100,000 population, more than doubled the national rate.

St. Louis is a city made up of 79 neighborhoods with well-defined and well-known boundaries. As might be expected, some of these neighborhoods have suffered the consequences of economic decline much more severely than others. Unemployment rates, poverty, and female-headed households all display their highest levels in a handful of neighborhoods clustered in the northern part of St. Louis. These areas, which are predominantly black, possess many of the physical signs commonly associated with urban decay: abandoned, boarded-up buildings, litter-strewn vacant lots, and gang graffiti sprayed on every available wall. There also is a visible streetlife, epitomized by the groups of young to middle-aged men who congregate on the corner, drinking, using drugs and, in their words, "kickin' it up." Women typically play a tangential role in these groups, though some are accepted as streetcorner regulars owing to their ability to "walk the walk and talk the talk" of this tough, male-dominated environment.

On the near south side of St. Louis, there are several neighborhoods traditionally populated by poor whites that also display the unmistakable features of urban disorder and decline. The streetlife in these neighborhoods, while bearing many similarities to that in the black areas, is organized around the "stoop" or front porch rather than the corner. Groups of young men and women can be seen sitting on the steps in front of their dilapidated residences, drinking beer, smoking marijuana, and otherwise "partying." Currently, these areas are undergoing substantial demographic change, with black in-migration and a notably high level of "white flight" in response.

Working in the neighborhoods described above, we located and interviewed 105 *currently active* offenders, focussing specifically on their thoughts and actions during the commission of their burglaries. The interviews were semi-structured and conducted in an informal manner, allowing the offenders to speak freely using their own words. This appeared to create a more relaxed atmosphere and raise the confidence and level of cooperation of the subjects. Interviews usually lasted between one and a half and three hours, with considerable time devoted to explaining questions and discussing answers. Our general impression was that the interviewees thought seriously about the questions put to them and responded truthfully. This is not to suggest that they never embellished their accounts in order to impress or mislead us. Almost certainly, some of them did so. Nevertheless, we do not believe that this happened often enough to undermine the overall validity of our data.

The truthfulness of what the offenders told us could be

monitored by questioning vague or inconsistent responses (see Wright and Bennett, 1990). Beyond this, we were able to check the arrest records of the 34 members of our sample who provided us with both a full name and a date of birth. This allowed us to compare what the offenders told us about prior arrests to their official arrest histories. As has been demonstrated for offenders in other research settings (e.g., West and Farrington, 1977), previous arrests generally were not underreported. Indeed, the results of this comparison indicated that, if anything, the burglars had *overreported* their arrests. The record check revealed that eight offenders had been arrested in the past; all but one of them also reported a previous arrest to us. Twenty of the 26 offenders for whom no prior arrests were found, however, nevertheless claimed to have been arrested previously. There are several plausible explanations for this apparent tendency to overreport past arrests. Perhaps the offenders failed to understand what it meant to be arrested, confusing being taken into custody or being stopped for questioning with an actual arrest. It also could be that some of them were last arrested as juveniles, in which case the arrests would not be included in the records made available to us. Finally, the arrest records themselves may well have been incomplete. Whatever the explanation, there is little reason to suspect that the offenders were purposely lying; there was no incentive for them to invent a previous arrest. Moreover, they took part in this research voluntarily and lying seems pointless when they could have declined to be interviewed in the first place (Glassner and Carpenter, 1985; Ianni, 1972).

We asked the offenders to tell us as much as they could about their most recent residential burglary. Throughout their description of this offense, we prompted them with further questions regarding such things as motivation, target selection, gaining entry to the dwelling, searching for valuables, and disposing of the goods. After the burglary had been described fully, we broke the crime down into its component parts and, for each part, asked the subjects whether this aspect of the offense was "typical" for them. If they answered that it was not, we asked them to describe a more typical situation. Our aim was to get a rich, complete overview of the way in which the offenders carried out their residential break-ins.

Additionally, we took 70 of the offenders to the site of a recent burglary for which they had not been apprehended and asked them to reconstruct the crime in considerable detail. By visiting targets, we could situate them in their neighborhood context. This allowed us to point out similar dwellings nearby, asking the offenders why they chose that particular residence in preference to these other places. Here, too, we questioned the subjects closely about the extent to which various elements of the offense described were typical of their break-ins. Thus, we were able to develop a clear picture of the ways in which the members of our sample *typically* went about committing their residential burglaries. It is that information that makes up the bulk of this book.

Characteristics of the Sample

The demographic characteristics of our sample are presented in table 1.

As can be seen, 72 of the offenders (69 percent) were black,

Table *1*. Demographic Characteristics of the Sample

Race	Number	Percentage	Sex	Number	Percentage
Black	72	69	Male	87	83
White	33	31	Female	18	17
	105	100		105	100

Age	Number	Percentage
Under 18	19	18
18 to 29	45	43
30 to 39	33	31
40 and over	8	8
	105	100

and the remaining 33 (31 percent) were white. In this respect, the sample is similar to the population of arrested burglary suspects for the City of St. Louis in 1988, the year immediately preceding our research. The St. Louis Metropolitan Police Department's Annual Report (1989) reveals that 64 percent of burglary arrestees in that year were black and 36 percent white. The sex distribution of our sample, on the other hand, differs greatly from that of the population of arrested burglary suspects in the city. Eighteen of the offenders we interviewed (17 percent) were female, whereas only 7 percent of the burglary arrestees in St. Louis in 1988 were female. This is not surprising. Given the statistical rarity of female burglars, we made a special effort to recruit enough of them to enable us to explore differences between their perspective and that of their male counterparts. As it turned out, however, these women did not approach their offenses much differently from the men (see Decker et al., 1993). In the rare cases where such a difference was found, this is made clear in the text.

Noteworthy is the fact that a substantial number of juveniles — 19 (18 percent of the total) — were located for the project. The inclusion of such offenders broadens the research considerably because many arrested residential burglars are under 18 years of age (Sessions, 1989). Juvenile offenders seldom are included in burglary studies that depend upon criminal justice channels because access to them is legally restricted and they often are processed differently than adult criminals and detained in separate facilities. It is interesting that, at the time we first interviewed them, 21 members of the sample admitted to being on probation or parole, or to be serving a suspended sentence.

Table 2 sets out whether, and to what degree, those in our sample have come into official contact with the criminal justice system.

Eight of the offenders, it can be seen, had never been arrested for any serious offense. We excluded arrests for traffic violations, "failure to appear," and similar minor transgressions because such offenses do not adequately distinguish seri-

Table 2. Contact with the Criminal Justice System

	Number	Percentage
Ever arrested	97	92
No arrests	8	8
	105	100

	Number	Percentage
No burglary arrests	44	42
Arrested for burglary, no convictions	35	33
Convicted of burglary	26	25
	105	100

ous criminals from others. These offenders would have been excluded had we based our study on a jail or prison population.

Perhaps a more relevant measure, however, is the experience of the offenders with the criminal justice system for burglary, because most previous studies of the burglar's perspective not only have been based on incarcerated offenders, but also have used the charge of burglary as a screen to select subjects (e.g., Bennett and Wright, 1984; Maguire and Bennett, 1982; Rengert and Wasilchick, 1985). Of the 105 offenders in our sample, 44 (42 percent) had no arrests for burglary, and another 35 (33 percent) had one or more arrests, but no convictions for the offense. Thus, three-quarters of our sample would not have been included in a study of incarcerated burglars. This puts us in a good position to be able to compare our results to those of earlier, prison-based investigations of the offender's perspective on residential burglary. As noted earlier, such a comparison is badly needed.

To determine how many residential burglaries the offenders had committed, we asked them to estimate the number of *completed* break-ins in which they had taken part. We "bounded" this response by posing three questions: (1) How old were they when they committed their first burglary? (2) Were there any significant gaps (e.g., periods of incarceration) in their offending? and (3) Had their level of offending fluctuated over time? The subjects typically offered a very rough estimate of how many burglaries they had committed, then were prompted with questions about variations in their rate of offending over the course of their criminal careers. In the end, we recorded what the offenders agreed was a conservative estimate of the number of lifetime burglaries. The responses to this question are summarized in table 3.

Approximately half of the sample (54 percent) admitted to 50 or more lifetime burglaries. (In cases where subjects estimated their total number of burglaries in terms of a range — e.g., 50 to 60 — we used the lower figure in our calculations.) Included in this group are 44 offenders who had committed at least 100 such crimes. At the other extreme are 11 individuals who had participated in nine or fewer residential break-ins.

The measure of lifetime burglaries, of course, does not provide an estimate of the *rate* of offending. For that, we calculated "lambda" (Blumstein and Cohen, 1979) — that is, the average number of burglaries per year — for each subject by using our interview data. We arrived at this figure by subtracting age at first burglary from age at the time of initial interview; from this, we subtracted the number of years each offender spent "off the street" in a secure residential facility (prison, jail, secure detention, or treatment center). This gave us the denominator for the lambda measure, the number of years at risk. The

---

Table 3. Number of Lifetime Burglaries

	Number of Offenders	Percentage*
Fewer than 10 burglaries	11	10
Between 10 and 49	37	35
Between 50 and 99	13	12
More than 99	44	42
	105	99

*Percentages do not total 100% due to rounding.

---

number of lifetime burglaries was divided by years at risk to get lambda. The results of this calculation are presented in table 4.

Two-thirds of the sample had averaged 10 or fewer burglaries a year over the course of their offending careers, a finding not out of line with lambda estimates for burglary derived from arrest data (Blumstein and Cohen, 1979). It must be noted, however, that there was great variability in the rate of offending across our sample: 33 percent committed, on average, fewer than five burglaries a year while, at the other end of the spectrum, 7 percent averaged 50 or more such crimes yearly.

During the course of our interviews, we asked the subjects whether they *ever* had committed other types of offenses besides residential burglary. The vast majority—83 of 105—admitted that they had. The crimes most often reported were theft (usually shoplifting), assault, and auto theft. We also asked many of the subjects whether they had taken part in offenses other than residential burglary during their *most recent* period of offending, usually the six months prior to being interviewed. Their responses are summarized in table 5.

As can be seen, many of them said they had committed other sorts of crimes during this time. These offenses included, among others, robbery, drug selling, and auto theft.

Table 4. Annual Number of Burglaries

	Number of Offenders	Percentage
Fewer than 5 burglaries per year	34	33
Between 5 and 10	34	33
Between 11 and 49	29	28
More than 49	7	7
	104*	101

*One offender was excluded from the analysis because necessary information was missing.

Table 5. Non-Burglary Offenses in Previous Six Months

	Number	*Percentage*
Theft	29	28
Auto theft	22	21
Drug possession	19	18
Drug sales	4	4
Robbery	14	13
Weapons violations	13	12
Assault	25	24
Prostitution	1	1
Disorderly conduct	13	12
Forgery	2	2
Fraud	5	5
Murder	6	6
Manslaughter	1	1
Kidnapping	1	1

Thus, while it may be convenient to think of these subjects as "residential burglars" for the purposes of the present study, it is important to remember that many of them are more criminally versatile than such a label implies. Indeed, few of the offenders in our sample referred to themselves as "burglars," preferring on the whole to be thought of as "hustlers," a term that reflects their ability to exploit a range of semi-legal and criminal opportunities (see Irwin, 1970; Tunnell, 1992). Nonetheless, a substantial minority of the subjects claimed they had *not* committed other types of crimes over the previous six months (excluding traffic violations and other minor offenses). These offenders might be considered residential burglary specialists, at least in the short term (Kempf, 1987).

Demographically, the sample was quite comprehensive, comprising offenders who were black and white, male and female, juvenile and adult, successful and unsuccessful, experienced and inexperienced, high-rate and low-rate, and specialist and nonspecialist. This was crucial in the context of our research, which aimed to encompass the diversity of views found among the population of criminals actively committing residential burglaries. The sample was homogeneous, however, in terms of socioeconomic status; it was composed almost entirely of the chronically poor, residents of the most seriously deprived north and south side inner-city neighborhoods of St. Louis. As Murray (1983) has noted, researchers have paid scant attention to the way in which lower-class offenders, especially those who victimize inner-city neighborhoods, perceive the social and physical environment of their crimes.

Locating the Subjects

We employed a "snowball" sampling strategy to locate the active offenders for our study. As described in the literature (e.g., Sudman, 1976; Watters and Biernacki, 1989), such a strategy begins with the recruitment of an initial subject who then is asked to refer further participants. This process continues until a suitable sample has been built. The most difficult aspect of researching active offenders using a snowball sampling technique is making that initial contact. Various ways of doing so have been suggested. McCall, for instance, recommends using a chain of referrals.

> If a researcher wants to make contact with, say, a bootlegger, he thinks of the person he knows who is closest in the social structure to bootlegging. Perhaps this person will be a police officer, a judge, a liquor store owner, a crime reporter, or a recently arrived Southern migrant. If he doesn't personally know a judge or a crime reporter, he surely knows someone (his own lawyer or a circulation clerk) who does and who would be willing to introduce him. By means of a very short chain of such referrals, the researcher can obtain an introduction to virtually any type of criminal. (McCall, 1978:31)

This strategy can be effective and efficient, but has pitfalls. To find active offenders for our study, we avoided seeking referrals from criminal justice officials for both practical and methodological reasons. From a practical standpoint, we elected not to use contacts from police or probation officers for fear that this would arouse the suspicions of offenders that the research was the front for a "sting" operation. In light of widespread media coverage of such operations, many active criminals are concerned about stings. One of the last offenders we interviewed, for example, explained that he had not agreed to participate earlier because he was worried about being set up for an arrest: "I thought about it at first because I've seen on T.V. telling how [the police] have sent letters out to people telling 'em they've won new sneakers and then arrested 'em." We also did not use referrals from law enforcement or corrections personnel to locate subjects because we were concerned that a sample obtained in this manner might be highly unrepresentative of active offenders. Such a sample likely would include a disproportionate number of unsuccessful criminals, that is, those who have been caught in the past (e.g., Hagedorn, 1990). By the same token, such a sample might exclude successful offenders who avoided associating with colleagues known to the police. Rengert and Wasilchick (1989:6), who used a probationer to contact active burglars, observed that the offenders so located "were often very much like the individual who led us to them."

By not relying on referrals from criminal justice sources, we compounded the difficulties inherent in trying to make initial contact with active offenders. A commonly-suggested alternative means of doing so involves frequenting locales favored by criminals (Chambliss, 1975; Polsky, 1969; West, 1980). This strategy, however, requires an extraordinary investment of time while the researcher establishes a street reputation as an "all right square" (Irwin, 1972:123) who can be trusted. Fortunately, we were able to short-cut the process by hiring an ex-offender (who, despite committing hundreds of serious crimes, had few arrests and no felony convictions) with high status among several groups of black street criminals in St. Louis. Our contact man had retired from crime after being shot and paralyzed in a gangland-style execution attempt. He then earned a bachelor's degree at our university, but continued to live in his old neighborhood, remaining friendly, albeit superficially, with local criminals. We met him when he disputed a speaker's characterization of street criminals during a colloquium in our department.

Working through an ex-offender with continuing ties to the underworld to locate active criminals has been used successfully by other criminologists (e.g., Taylor, 1985). Such a person has established contacts and trust in the criminal subculture and can vouch for the legitimacy of the research. To exploit this advantage fully, however, the contact must be someone with a solid street reputation for integrity. As Walker and Lidz (1977:115) have pointed out: "If access is needed, the individual who will establish the [researcher's] credentials must be well thought of by the other participants in the system." Further, this person must have a strong commitment to the goals of the study. Criminals, after all, recognize that researchers can be gullible and may try to enlist the ex-offender's help in deceiving them.

The ex-offender hired to locate subjects for our project began by approaching former criminal associates. Some of these contacts were still actively involved in various types of crimes, whereas others either had retired or remained involved only peripherally through, for example, occasional buying and selling of stolen goods. Only two of those initially approached were—or ever had been—burglars themselves. Shortly thereafter, the ex-offender contacted several streetwise law-abiding friends, including a youth worker. He explained the research to the contacts, stressing that it was confidential and that the police were not involved. He also informed them that those who agreed to be interviewed for the project would be paid a small sum (typically $25, though some received up to $50). He then asked the contacts to put him in touch with offenders actively involved in committing residential burglaries.

Figure 1 outlines the networks through which the offenders were located.

Perhaps the best way to clarify the recruitment process is to select a subject, say 064 (located at the bottom of the figure, just to the left of center), and identify the referrals that led us

Figure 1

"SNOWBALL" REFERRAL CHART

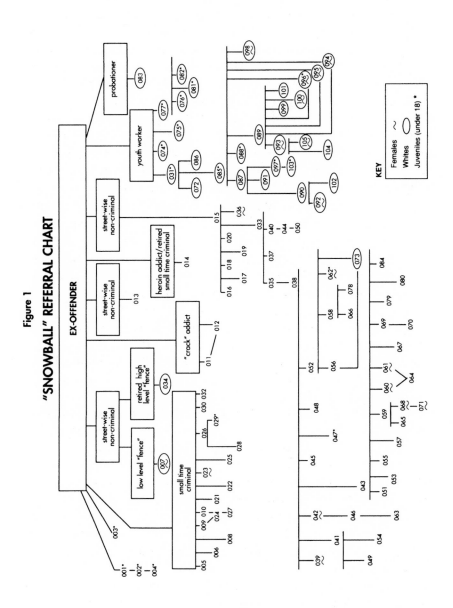

to this person. In this case, the ex-offender working on our project contacted a streetwise, noncriminal acquaintance who put him in touch with the first active offender in the chain, 015. Offender 015 referred seven colleagues, one of whom— 033—put us in touch with three more subjects, including 035. Offender 035 in turn introduced us to 038 who referred eight more participants. Among them was offender 043, a well-connected burglar who provided us with twelve further contacts, two of whom—060 and 061—convinced 064 to participate in the research. (As figure 1 makes obvious, it was not unusual for two offenders to refer the same person.) This procedure is similar to that described by Watters and Biernacki (1989:426) in that "the majority of respondents were not referred directly by the research staff." Instead, respondents came to us through the efforts of various actors in the street scene such as drug addicts, small-time criminals, and fences for stolen goods. We almost certainly would not have been able to find many of these individuals on our own, let alone convince them to cooperate.

As can be seen, the referral networks themselves tended strongly toward racial homogeneity. No white offender provided a black referral, while just two blacks jointly referred the same white burglar. More than anything, this probably reflects the extreme racial polarization that characterizes St. Louis generally. That polarization made it difficult for the black ex-offender employed on this research to locate white burglars. His former criminal associates had little to do with white offenders and thus they could not offer much help in contacting them. Indeed, it was only through the ex-offender's willingness to impose on the friendship of a local youth worker, herself black, that he was able to get a substantial number of initial introductions to white burglars. These subjects, all of whom were juveniles, were known to the youth worker because they formerly had been clients, referred to her office for various behavioral problems. The referral networks were far more heterogeneous in regard to sex; males often put us in contact with females and, occasionally, females referred us to males. The fact that the project fieldworker was male did not appear to hinder his ability to locate women burglars through references provided by other offenders.

The representativeness of a sample drawn from criminals at large in the community can never be determined conclusively because the parameters of the total population are unknown (Glassner and Carpenter, 1985; Watters and Biernacki, 1989). In constructing our sample, we sought primarily to encompass, insofar as possible, the diversity of perspectives on committing residential burglaries found among the population of active offenders. To do so, we initiated the sampling through ten different street contacts, thereby reducing the chances of tapping into just one or two criminal networks consisting of like-minded offenders. Further, we questioned subjects extensively about the ways in which their views might differ from those held by other offenders in their social circle. When such differences were noted, we made a concerted effort to convince interviewees to refer to us those holding disparate perspectives. Such measures, while not foolproof—the views of offenders outside of the penetrated networks, for example, will remain unknown—undoubtedly enhanced the representativeness of our sample. It must be remembered that virtually all of the offenders we contacted were poor, inner-city residents. Certainly our results should not be generalized to the (perhaps rare) persistent middle-class, suburban burglar. That said, it is worth mentioning that some members of our sample themselves travelled to the suburbs to offend, and a few were highly skilled and professional in their approach to committing residential burglaries. The views expressed by these offenders may not be markedly different from those of their middle-class counterparts, at least in regard to some issues (e.g., target selection). This, however, is a matter of conjecture.

We encountered numerous difficulties and challenges throughout the process of locating subjects. Figure 2 graphically illustrates how the recruitment of subjects waxed and waned over the course of the research.

A variety of factors were responsible for our uneven progress

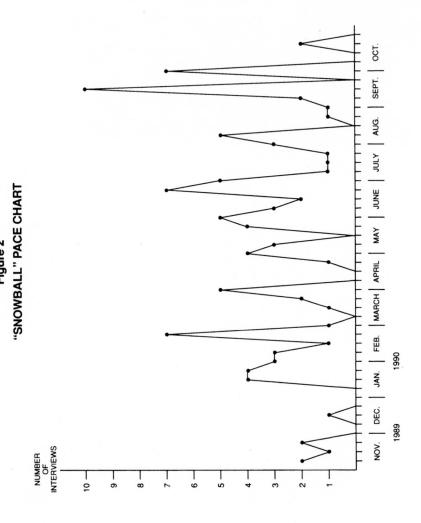

Figure 2
"SNOWBALL" PACE CHART

in locating offenders. Certainly the vicissitudes of the St. Louis winter played a part; it was difficult to recruit participants during periods of heavy rain, snow, or extreme cold. The prevailing level of the project fieldworker's enthusiasm also influenced the process of finding offenders. Ironically, successful bursts of recruiting had a tendency to cause him to become tired and "burned out," culminating in a period of reduced activity during which he devoted little effort to locating further subjects. These periods of lethargy typically lasted until we promised to reward the fieldworker with a first-rate Italian dinner upon the recruitment of a set number of additional participants.

Beyond these problems, we faced the predictable difficulties common to virtually all fieldwork involving hidden or deviant populations. Contacts that initially appeared to be promising, for instance, sometimes proved to be unproductive and had to be dropped. And, of course, even productive contact chains had a tendency to dry up in time. One of the most challenging tasks we confronted involved what Biernacki and Waldorf (1981:150) have termed the "verification of eligibility," that is, determining whether potential subjects actually met the criteria for inclusion in our research. Offenders had to be both "residential burglars" and "currently active." In theory, this meant that they had to have committed a residential burglary within the past two weeks. This eligibility requirement seems straightforward, but it often was difficult to apply in the field because many offenders were evasive about their crimes. In such cases, we frequently had to rely on the ex-offender and other members of the sample to verify the eligibility of potential subjects. In fact, a few of those taking part in the project had last offended outside of our original two-week time limit. Subjects who clearly (1) saw themselves as being currently active and (2) were regarded as such by other offenders occasionally were included because it seemed ill-advised to turn away potentially valuable respondents for the sake of adhering to what was, after all, an arbitrary operational definition in the first place. We were flexible about this limit particularly in cases where the offenders concerned were of special interest to us because they were unlike most of the other burglars in our sample (e.g., never apprehended for anything, female).

We did not pay the contacts to help us to find subjects and, initially, motivating them to do so proved difficult. There is a saying on the street that "money talks and bullshit walks," an expression that neatly captures the general reluctance of our informants to do something for nothing. Small favors, things like giving them a ride or buying them a pack of cigarettes, produced some cooperation, but yielded only a few introductions. Moreover, the active offenders that we did manage to interview often were lackadaisical about referring associates because no financial incentive was offered. Eventually, one of the informants hit on the idea of "pimping" colleagues, that is, arranging an introduction on their behalf in exchange for a cut of the participation fee (see Cromwell et al., 1991). This idea was adopted rapidly by other informants and the number of referrals rose accordingly. In effect, these informants became "locators" (Biernacki and Waldorf, 1981:152), helping us to expand referral networks as well as vouching for the legitimacy of the research, and validating potential participants as active residential burglars.

We had no hand in the initial development of the pimping scheme; it operated clandestinely for some time before we learned of its existence. The practice first came to our attention when we picked up an offender referred by an informer, only to find that the informant expected to be allowed to come along and sit in on the interview. We explained that for reasons of confidentiality this was not possible and, thus, he and the interviewee agreed to meet at a designated spot afterwards. At the conclusion of the interview, however, the subject asked to be dropped off at a different location. When we reminded him that he had arranged to meet up with the informant, he replied testily: "I put myself on the line for this twenty-five dollars . . . I'm not giving him shit." As we questioned him further about this, it emerged that other informants also demanded an "introduction fee," typically $10, from the offenders they referred to us.

The practice of pimping is consistent with the low level, underworld economy of street culture, where people are always looking for a way to get in on someone else's deal. One of our contacts put it this way: "If there's money to make out of something, I gotta figure out a way to get me some of it." We made no attempt to discourage the pimping arrangement; indeed, as the rate of referrals declined toward the end of the fieldwork, we unwittingly encouraged the practice by increasing the initial interview payment to $50. This was done to induce the more reluctant burglars—those who might approach offenses quite differently than their less cautious counterparts—to see us, but it also acted as an incentive to informants who envisioned a chance to charge offenders a higher referral fee.

Over the course of the research, numerous disputes arose between offenders and informants regarding the payment of referral fees. We resisted becoming involved in these disputes, reckoning that our involvement could only result in the alienation of one or both parties (e.g., Miller, 1952). Instead, we made it clear that our funds were intended as interview payments and would be given only to interviewees.

Field Relations

The success of our research hinged on our ability to convince potential subjects to participate. This required considerable delicacy, as many of the active burglars, especially those we located early in the project, were deeply suspicious of our motives. Given such suspicion, it is reasonable to ask why they were willing to take part in the research. Certainly the fact that we paid them a small sum was an enticement for many, but this is not an adequate explanation. Criminal opportunities abound and even the inept "nickel and dime" offenders in the sample could have earned more if they had spent the time engaged in illegal activity. And, from their perspective, crime, at least initially, may have appeared to be the less risky moneymaking venture. Moreover, some of the participants clearly were not short of cash. This was dramatically illustrated when, at the close of an interview, an offender pulled out his wallet to show us that it was stuffed with thousand dollar bills. He explained: "I didn't do this for the money . . . I did it to help out [the ex-offender employed on our project]. We know some of the same people and he said you were cool." Nevertheless, he did not hesitate to take the $25 interview payment.

Without doubt, others in our sample also agreed to participate because the ex-offender assured them that we were trustworthy. But additional factors were at work. Letkemann (1973:44), among others, has observed that the secrecy inherent in criminal work means that offenders have few opportunities to discuss their activities with anyone besides associates, a matter which many find frustrating. As one of Letkemann's informants put it: "What's the point of scoring if nobody knows about it." Under the right conditions, therefore, some offenders enjoy talking about their achievements with researchers. Our research, as noted, sought to understand the world of burglary from the offender's perspective; it treated the subjects as having expert knowledge normally unavailable to outsiders. Such a strategy engages the cooperation of offenders who, not surprisingly, desire social recognition for their competence in much the same way as do law-abiding citizens (West, 1980). The ex-offender had informed potential interviewees that we planned to write a book based on our research and many of them clearly were pleased by this prospect. They viewed the opportunity to be in a book, albeit anonymously, as a powerful acknowledgment of their competence. We were frequently reminded of this fact during the time it took us to produce a manuscript, receiving several calls a month from offenders asking when the book would be published and where they could buy a copy.

Beyond this, we adopted several further strategies to maximize cooperation. First, following the recommendations of a number of experienced field researchers (e.g., Irwin, 1972; Mc-Call, 1978; Walker and Lidz, 1977; Wright and Bennett, 1990), we made an effort to fit in by learning the distinctive terminology and phrasing used by the offenders. Here again, the assistance of the ex-offender proved invaluable. Prior to entering the field, he had suggested ways in which questions might be asked so that the subjects would better understand them, and had provided us with a vocabulary of popular street terms (e.g., "boy" for heroin, "girl" for cocaine) and pronunciations (e.g., "hair ron" for heroin). What is more, he sat in on the early interviews and critiqued them afterwards, noting areas of difficulty or contention and offering possible solutions. In attempting to deal with the offenders we did not try to be one of them. As Hagedorn (1990:253) has noted, such attempts are doomed to failure: "Trying to act like an insider . . . is phony, and the data reported will inevitably be phony" (see also Whyte, 1981). Rather, we strove to create a comfortable interview situation built on a solid foundation of shared meanings.

A second strategy to gain the cooperation of the offenders required us to give as well as take. We expected the subjects to answer our questions frankly and, therefore, often had to reciprocate. Almost all of the burglars had questions about how the information would be used, who would have access to it, and similar kinds of inquiries (see Glassner and Carpenter, 1985). We answered these questions honestly. Further, we honored requests from a number of subjects for various forms of assistance. Like most street criminals, those in our sample tended to lead problematic lives and, over the course of the fieldwork, frequently required help. Provided that the help was legal and fell within the general set "of norms governing the exchange of money and other kinds of favors" (Berk and Adams, 1970:112) on the street, we offered it. We occasionally "loaned" offenders small amounts of money, though never more than a few dollars. None of these loans were repaid. We took subjects to job interviews or work, helped some to enroll in school, and gave others advice on legal matters. We also assisted a juvenile offender injured while running away from the police to arrange for emergency surgery when his parents, fearing that they would be charged for the operation, refused to provide their consent.

The third, and final, way in which we sought to obtain and keep the confidence of the offenders involved demonstrating our trustworthiness by "remaining close-mouthed in regard to potentially harmful information" (Irwin, 1972:125). Understandably, the subjects were concerned that we not divulge data that were incriminating or otherwise confidential. In an apparent attempt to reassure themselves, a number of the offenders tested us by asking what a criminal associate said about a particular matter. We declined to discuss such issues, hard though it sometimes was, explaining that the promise of confidentiality extended to all those participating in our research.

Much has been written about the necessity for researchers to withstand official coercion (see, e.g., Irwin, 1972; McCall, 1978; Polsky, 1969) and we recognized from the start the threat that intrusions from criminal justice personnel could pose to our research. The risk of being confronted by police patrols seemed especially great since we planned to visit the site of recent successful burglaries with offenders. We significantly reduced this possibility before beginning our fieldwork by negotiating an agreement with the police that they would not interfere in our research. Cromwell et al. (1991) maintain that, without an agreement of this sort, field studies of active criminals may well be impossible. Negotiating such an agreement, however, is not always easy. But the fact that we had a good working relationship with the police, built up over many years, made it possible for us to achieve cooperation. Once again, though, we were short-cutting a process that could take a researcher without police connections a great deal of time. As a further precaution, we sent information that could identify participants by name or link them to a specific offense to an address in the United Kingdom, where it was held by a British colleague beyond the reach of any subpoena that might be issued in the United States.

The strategies described above helped to overcome the problems inherent in working with active criminals (e.g., Dunlap et al., 1990); nonetheless, we encountered many potentially dangerous situations during the research period. Offenders turned up for interviews carrying firearms, including a machine gun on one occasion; we were challenged on the street by subjects who feared that they were being set up for arrest; we were caught in the middle of a fight over the payment of a $1 debt. Probably the most dangerous situation, however, arose while driving with an offender to the site of his most recent burglary. As we passed a pedestrian, the offender became agitated and demanded that we stop the car: "You want to see me kill someone? Stop the car! I'm gonna kill that motherfucker. Stop the fuckin' car!" We refused to stop and speeded up to prevent him from jumping out of the vehicle. This clearly displeased him, but he eventually calmed down and allowed us to complete the visit to the burglary site. When and where such explosive situations would develop was largely unpredictable. Often we deferred to the ex-offender's judgment about the safety of a given set of circumstances. For example, we were parked in front of a "crack house" with two burglars who were describing how they had broken into the place and stolen cash, drugs and weapons. As we talked, four teenage males came out of the house, walked slowly past our car, and stopped about 100 yards behind us. When they headed back a minute or two later, the ex-offender, who had been watching them intently in the rearview mirror, said, "It's time to get out of here. They're gonna shoot us." We will never know whether he was right; we left without delay. The most notable precaution we took was to make sure the offenders knew that we carried little more money than was necessary to pay them. This not only made us feel safer from the threat of being robbed, it also helped to hold down the sums requested as loans to no more than a few dollars.

Not all the difficulties that we encountered on the streets were created by the offenders; the project fieldworker—who, after all, bridged legitimate society and the criminal underworld—sometimes failed to follow stipulated procedures and had to be reminded of the importance of adhering to legal and ethical standards. On one occasion, for instance, we were riding in the back seat of the fieldworker's car when we heard him mention to the offender sitting in front that he did not have any auto insurance. We immediately terminated our research for the day, gave the fieldworker some money and told him to get insurance. He assured us that he would do so right away, adding, "but first I have to get a driver's license."

Data Collection and Analysis

Our semi-structured interviews were tape-recorded, with the permission of each offender, as were conversations held during visits to the scenes of recent residential burglaries. None of the interviewees objected to being taped. The tapes were transcribed verbatim using a personal computer, with identification tags corresponding to relevant research issues inserted in the transcripts. The tags allowed us, with the help of "GOFER"—a simple qualitative data software package—to retrieve all the comments made by the offenders about various predetermined matters. The issues that the tags covered generally were quite broad (e.g., motivation, target selection), leaving a great deal of scope for a more detailed analysis directed toward establishing "within issue" variations from one offense to the next or, more often, from one offender to another. We carried out this fine-grained analysis by reading the lists of comments and, for each issue, creating categories that captured distinctions recognized by the offenders themselves as being relevant.

By tagging the data, we were constructing an analytical framework that reflected our interest in matters relating to the process of committing residential burglaries. In effect, we were deciding "what to tell and how to tell it" (Van Maanen, 1988:25) because untagged information would not readily be available for analysis. While such decisions are inevitable, the rationale underlying them must be stated explicitly. In devising our tagging scheme, we were influenced by two analytical approaches that, at first glance, may seem to be strange bedfellows for the study of crime: rational choice theory (Clarke and Cornish, 1985; Cornish and Clarke, 1986) and phenomenological interactionism (Katz, 1988; Lofland, 1969). Both approaches focus on the immediate circumstances surrounding the commission of crimes and emphasize the situational and sequential nature of offender decision making. Rational choice theory, however, views criminal decision making as deliberate and calculating, involving at least a rudimentary weighing of the available options at various points throughout the course of offenses in an attempt to determine the "optimal action" at critical moments in time (Coleman and Fararo, 1992:xi). As such, it stresses the objective factors that shape offenders' decisions during the commission of their crimes. Phenomenological interactionism, on the other hand, sees crimes as emerging almost naturally from the flow of events, often occurring without substantial planning or deliberation beforehand. Accordingly, it emphasizes the subjective factors that impel individuals toward offending. By combining these two analytical approaches, we sought to examine not only the hard, verifiable contingencies (e.g., risks, rewards, physical obstacles) that influenced the way in which offenders carried out their burglaries, but also the impact of mood, intuition, beliefs in magic, and superstition (Shover, 1991; Walsh, 1986). Until now, researchers have tended to employ one approach to the exclusion of the other; in real life, though, the two must interact in shaping the perceptions of criminals (Scheff, 1992). Our goal was to establish empirically both the nature of this interaction and the explanatory limits of each analytical approach individually. In short, we sought to gain a realistic understanding of the "psychological springs" that underpinned the actions of the offenders during their crimes (Coleman and Fararo, 1992:x). This necessitated an analytical framework that broke down the burglars' offenses into distinct stages — or "sequential events" (Scheff, 1990:195) — thereby allowing us to explore objective and subjective aspects of the situation that guided their actions throughout criminal episodes. As Lofland (1969:61), among others, has argued, such descriptive, "close-up" information is of critical importance in formulating an adequate explanation of a crime such as residential burglary (see also Cornish and Clarke, 1986; Katz, 1988; Scheff, 1990). Notably, it can illuminate the links between the overall lifestyles and daily activities of offenders and specific instances of lawbreaking. Criminal decision making, after all, must be embedded in and subject to the influences of a wider cultural context (Kennedy and Baron, 1993). Hagan and McCarthy (1992:556), for example, have shown that exposure to "street-life," in and of itself, "is productive of serious delinquency." However, it remains unclear "exactly what aspects of life on the street cause delinquency." The present study is well suited to a preliminary exploration of this issue, at least in regard to offenses of residential burglary. What is more, by demonstrating the conditions and mechanisms that make these offenses possible, this study also should be able to pinpoint ways of making them less likely (Glassner and Carpenter, 1985; Johnson et al., 1993). For instance, it might help to explain the apparent ability of offenders to overcome the deterrence potential of threatened sanctions. And it might shed light on the extent to which such threats play a part in circumscribing their activities during the commission of residential burglaries.

In the chapters that follow, we will present an "offender's eye view" of how residential burglaries are carried out and what it feels like to commit them. In keeping with the spirit of our analytical scheme, the chapters have been arranged sequentially, taking the reader through the steps required to commit such a crime. Chapter 2 examines the circumstances under which offenders become motivated to burglarize a dwelling. Chapter 3 considers how and why they select particular targets. The process by which offenders actually break into targets is explored in chapter 4. Chapter 5 discusses the strategies burglars employ when searching residences, while chapter 6 looks at the ways in which they dispose of stolen goods. The implications of our findings, both for criminological theory and research and for crime prevention policy, will be considered fully in chapter 7. Chapters 2 through 6 make extensive use of quoted material drawn from the offenders. It must be stressed, however, that this material was chosen *by us* to illustrate *our interpretation* of the offender's perspective on residential burglary. Van Maanen has poked fun at researchers who do not acknowledge their role in "framing" or "contextualizing" what he calls the native's point of view:

> Quotes are redundant, staged and of course closely edited to embellish the [researcher's] methodical observations and analytical categories with native jargon. The result is that the interested interpretations of the members themselves seem to overlap and comprise the analysis itself — "It's not my perspective," says the author, "but theirs." The native's point of view is thus put forward. (Van Maanen, 1988:64)

The bottom line is that we necessarily had a hand in shaping our representation of the offender's perspective. (How could it be otherwise?) Obviously, this created the possibility that misinterpretations and distortions might creep into the text. To keep this to a minimum, we did something seldom done in criminological research; as the writing proceeded, we read various parts of the manuscript to selected members of the sample. This allowed us to check our interpretations against those of insiders and to enlist their help in reformulating passages they regarded as misleading or inaccurate. In essence, we submitted our evidence for trial, a procedure recommended by Scheff as being far superior to the more usual interpretive schemes employed in either quantitative or qualitative social science research:

> If we leave academic research, however, many approaches may be used to interpret ambiguous texts. In courts of law, for example, disputants freely interpret verbatim texts. But these interpretations are neither discounted as being merely subjective nor accepted on faith. Rather they are considered

merely as one step in a round of interpretations and counter-interpretations, a round that will continue until consensus is reached. (Scheff, 1992:110)

The result of using this procedure, we believe, is a book that faithfully conveys the offender's perspective on the process of committing residential burglaries.

Two further caveats are in order. First, although we made a concerted effort to question every offender about every issue, this was not always possible; in consequence, the number of offenders responding to a question varies from one issue to the next. For the major response categories, the number of offenders speaking to the matter under scrutiny has been noted. Second, quotations have not been edited to correct grammar, except where this was necessary to make the meaning clear. Bracketed text indicates the addition or substitution of a word or words. Indented quotes have been linked to the offenders responsible for them through the use of a self-assigned alias (given only on the first occasion on which a particular burglar is quoted) plus a three digit code number (see Appendix for descriptive information on each respondent). Other quotes have not been attributed to specific individuals because, quite frankly, a number of them were culled from hastily recorded field notes relating to casual, non-interview conversations. As Van Maanen (1988:56–57) has noted, such mistakes are inevitable given the enormity of the fieldwork enterprise. Indeed, he maintains that admitting them can "help to establish the fieldworker's credibility," adding that absent any evidence of fallibility, "the fieldworker might appear too perfect and thus strain the reader's good faith." We are not being falsely modest in asserting that the good faith of those reading this book should not be challenged unduly.

2

Deciding to Commit a Burglary

THE DEMOGRAPHIC CHARACTERISTICS of residential burglars have been well documented. As Shover (1991) has observed, such offenders are, among other things, disproportionately young, male, and poor. These characteristics serve to identify a segment of the population more prone than others to resort to breaking in to dwellings, but they offer little insight into the actual causes of residential burglary. Many poor, young males, after all, never commit any sort of serious offense, let alone a burglary. And even those who carry out such crimes are not offending most of the time. This is not, by and large, a continually motivated group of criminals; the motivation for them to offend is closely tied to their assessment of current circumstances and prospects. The direct cause of residential burglary is a perceptual process through which the offense comes to be seen as a means of meeting an immediate need, that is, through which a motive for the crime is formed.

Walker (1984:viii) has pointed out that, in order to develop a convincing explanation for criminal behavior, we must begin by "distinguishing the states of mind in which offenders commit, or contemplate the commission of, their offenses." Similarly, Katz (1988:4), arguing for increased research into what he calls the foreground of criminality, has noted that all of the demographic information on criminals in the world cannot answer the following question: "Why are people who were not determined to commit a crime one moment determined to do so the next?" This is the question to which the present chapter is addressed. The aim is to explore the extent to which the decision to commit a residential burglary is the result of a process of careful calculation and deliberation.

In the overwhelming majority of cases, the decision to commit a residential burglary arises in the face of what offenders perceive to be a pressing need for cash. Previous research consistently has shown this to be so (Bennett and Wright, 1984; Cromwell et al., 1991) and the results of the present study bear out this point. More than nine out of ten of the offenders in our sample — 95 of 102 — reported that they broke into dwellings primarily when they needed money.

> Well, it's like, the way it clicks into your head is like, you'll be thinking about something and, you know, it's a problem. Then it, like, all relates. "Hey, I need some money! Then how am I going to get money? Well, how do you know how to get money quick and easy?" Then there it is. Next thing you know, you are watching [a house] or calling to see if [the occupants] are home. (Wild Will — No. 010)

> Usually when I get in my car and drive around I'm thinking, I don't have any money, so what is my means for gettin' money? All of a sudden I'll just take a glance and say, "There it is! There's the house" . . . Then I get this feelin', that right moment, I'm movin' then. (Larry William — No. 017)

These offenders were not motivated by a desire for money for its own sake. By and large, they were not accumulating the capital needed to achieve a long-range goal. Rather, they regarded money as providing them with the means to solve an immediate problem. In their view, burglary was a matter of day-to-day survival.

> I didn't have the luxury of laying back in no damn pinstriped [suit]. I'm poor and I'm raggedy and I need some food and I need some shoes . . . So I got to have some money some kind of way. If it's got to be the wrong way, then so be it. (Mark Smith—No. 030)

> When I first started out, when I was younger, [burglary] was excitement or a high. But now it's to get by, you know, to survive. I don't ask my father for anything. My mother is not able to help. (Larry Harris—No. 035)

Given this view, it is unsurprising that the frequency with which the offenders committed burglaries was governed largely by the amount of money in their pockets. Many of them would not offend so long as they had sufficient cash to meet current expenses.

> Usually what I'll do is a burglary, maybe two or three if I have to, and then this will help me get over the rough spot until I can get my shit straightened out. Once I get it straightened out, I just go with the flow until I hit that rough spot where I need the money again. And then I hit it . . . the only time I would go and commit a burglary is if I needed the money at that point in time. That would be strictly to pay light bill, gas bill, rent. (Dan Whiting—No. 102)

> Long as I got some money, I'm cool. If I ain't got no money and I want to get high, then I go for it. (Janet Wilson—No. 060)

> You know how they say stretch a dollar? I'll stretch it from here to the parking lot. But I can only stretch it so far and then it breaks. Then I say, "Well, I guess I got to go put on my black clothes. Go on out there like a thief in the night." (Ralph Jones—No. 018)

A few of the offenders sometimes committed a burglary even though they had sufficient cash for their immediate needs. These subjects were not purposely saving money, but they were unwilling to pass up opportunities to make more. They attributed their behavior to having become "greedy" or "addicted" to money.

> I have done it out of greed, per se. Just to be doing it and to have more money, you know? Say, for instance, I have two hundred dollars in my pocket now. If I had two more hundreds, then that's four hundred dollars. Go out there and do a burglary. Then I say, "If I have four hundred dollars, then I can have a thousand." Go out there and do a burglary. (No. 018)

> It's like when you smoke a cigarette, you know, you want more and more from the nicotine. Well, from my experience, you can get bigger and better stuff the more times that you do it and you can make more money. I'm addicted to money, I love money. So I just keep doing [burglaries]. (Robert Jones—No. 103)

Typically, the offenders did not save the money that they derived through burglary. Instead, they spent it for one or more of the following purposes: (1) to "keep the party going"; (2) to keep up appearances; or (3) to keep themselves and their families fed, clothed, and sheltered.

Keeping the Party Going

Although the offenders often stated that they committed residential burglaries to "survive," there is a danger in taking this claim at face value. When asked how they spent the proceeds of their burglaries, nearly three-quarters of them—68 of 95—said they used the money for various forms of (for want of a better term) high-living. Most commonly, this involved the use of illicit drugs. Fifty-nine of the 68 offenders who spent the money obtained from burglary on pleasure-seeking pursuits specifically mentioned the purchase of drugs. For many of these respondents, the decision to break into a dwelling often arose as a result of a heavy session of drug use. The objective was to get the money to keep the party going (Shover and Honaker, 1990). The drug most frequently implicated in these situations was "crack" cocaine.

> [Y]ou ever had an urge before? Maybe a cigarette urge or a food urge, where you eat that and you got to have more and more? That's how that crack is. You smoke it and it hits you [in the back of the throat] and you got to have more. I'll smoke that sixteenth up and get through, it's like I never had none. I got to have more. Therefore, I gots to go do another burglary and gets some more money. (Richard Jackson—No. 009)

> It's usually, say we'll be doing some coke and then you really want more, so we'll go and do [a burglary] and get some money. (Sasha Williams—No. 094)

> I might find somebody with some good crack . . . while I'm high I say, "Damn, I want me some more of this shit!" Go knock a place off, make some more money, go buy some more dope. (Die Leo—No. 079)

Lemert (1953:304) has labelled situations like these "dialectical, self-enclosed systems of behavior" in that they have an internal logic or "false structure" which calls for more of the same. Once locked into such events, he asserts, participants experience considerable pressure to continue, even if this involves breaking the law.

> A man away from home who falls in with a group of persons who have embarked upon a two or three-day or even a week's period of drinking and carousing . . . tends to have the impetus to continue the pattern which gets mutually reinforced by [the] interaction of the participants, and [the pattern] tends to have an accelerated beginning, a climax and a terminus. If midway through a spree a participant runs

out of money, the pressures immediately become critical to take such measures as are necessary to preserve the behavior sequence. A similar behavior sequence is [evident] in that of the alcoholic who reaches a "high point" in his drinking and runs out of money. He might go home and get clothes to pawn or go and borrow money from a friend or even apply for public relief, but these alternatives become irrelevant because of the immediacy of his need for alcohol. (Lemert, 1953:303)

Implicit in this explanation is an image of actors who become involved in offending without significant calculation; having embarked voluntarily on one course of action (e.g., crack smoking), they suddenly find themselves being drawn into an unanticipated activity (e.g., residential burglary) as a means of sustaining that action. Their offending is not the result of a thoughtful, carefully reasoned process. Instead, it emerges as part of the natural flow of events, seemingly coming out of nowhere. In other words, it is not so much that these actors consciously choose to commit crimes as that they elect to get involved in situations that drive them toward lawbreaking (Kennedy and Baron, 1993).

Other subjects, though they claimed that a perceived need for drugs typically triggered their decision to do a burglary, were not under the influence of drugs when the decision was reached. Their aim was to get high rather than to stay high. They regarded themselves as having a drug "habit" which compelled them to crime; the urge for drugs seemed beyond their ability to control and had to be satisfied by whatever means necessary. Although some in this group were addicted to narcotics such as heroin, this was not always the case.

See, sometimes I wake up and don't have no [marijuana]. I have to go do my [burglary] and get me some money and get me some. (Carl Jackson—No. 022)

Getting and using drugs were major preoccupations for a majority of the offenders, not just a small cadre of addicts. Many of them reported committing burglaries *solely* for the purpose of obtaining money to buy drugs. But even some of those who did burglaries for other reasons ended up spending a portion of the profits on drugs.

> Lot of times when I commit burglary I use some of the money to get drugs, but I don't do the burglaries for that purpose. (Larry Washington—No. 013)

For these offenders, indulgence in drug use represented a crucial aspect of their street identity as "hip"; the streetcorner culture from which most of them—black and white, male and female—were drawn is oriented largely toward getting high (Anderson, 1990). In the past, this almost exclusively involved the drinking of beer or cheap wine. While drinking remains a feature of street culture—14 offenders, 21 percent of those who spent their money on high-living, mentioned the purchase of alcohol—it is increasingly being accompanied by illicit drug use. The money required to support such use is substantial and this ensured that the offenders were almost perpetually in need of cash (Shover and Honaker, 1992).

Beyond the purchase of illicit drugs and, to a lesser extent, alcohol, 10 of the 68 offenders—15 percent—also used the proceeds from their residential burglaries to pursue sexual conquests. All of these offenders were male. Some liked to flash money about, believing that this was the way to attract women.

> I guess I like to flash [money] a lot, impress the girls and stuff. Go out and spend some money, you know? (Wayne Jones—No. 055)

> [I commit burglaries to] splurge money with the women, you know, that's they kick, that's what they like to do. (Jon Monroe—No. 011)

> [I use the burglary money for] gifts for young ladies — flowers or negligee or somethin'. Some shoes, "Put them shoes on,

them pumps." [Then] watch 'em nude. (Jack Daniel—No. 054)

Like getting high, sexual conquest was a much-prized symbol of hipness through which the male subjects in our sample could accrue status among their peers on the street. The greatest prestige was accorded to those who were granted sexual favors solely on the basis of smooth talk and careful impression management. Nevertheless, a few of the offenders took a more direct approach to obtaining sex by paying a streetcorner prostitute (sometimes referred to as a "duck") for it. While this was regarded as less hip than the more subtle approach described above, it had the advantage of being easy and uncomplicated. As such, it appealed to offenders who were wrapped up in partying and therefore reluctant to devote more effort than was necessary to satisfy their immediate sexual desires.

I spend [the money] on something to drink, . . . then get me some [marijuana]. Then I'm gonna find me a duck. (Ricky Davis—No. 015)

It would be misleading to suggest that any of the offenders we spoke to committed burglaries *specifically* to get money for sex, but a number of them often directed a portion of their earnings toward this goal.

In short, among the major purposes for which the offenders used the money derived from burglary was the maintenance of a lifestyle centered on illicit drugs, but frequently incorporating alcohol and sexual conquests as well. This lifestyle reflects the values of the street culture, a culture characterized by an openness to "illicit action" (Katz, 1988:209–15), to which most of our subjects were strongly committed. Viewed from the perspective of the offenders, then, the oft-heard claim that they broke into dwellings to survive does not seem quite so farfetched. The majority of them saw their fate as inextricably linked to an ability to fulfill the imperatives of life on the street.

Keeping Up Appearances

Of the 95 offenders who committed residential burglaries primarily for financial reasons, 43 reported that they used the cash to purchase various "status" items. The most popular item was clothing; 39 of the 43 said that they bought clothes with the proceeds of their crimes. At one level, of course, clothing must be regarded as necessary for survival. The responses of most of the offenders, however, left little doubt that they were not buying clothes to protect themselves from the elements, but rather to project a certain image; they were drawn to styles and brand names regarded as chic on the streets.

> See, I go steal money and go buy me some clothes. See, I likes to look good. I likes to dress. All I wear is Stacy Adams, that's all I wear. [I own] only one pair of blue jeans cause I likes to dress. (No. 011)

> I buy fashionable clothes or whatever, you know, just spend [the money]. (Mike West—No. 049)

> [I] buy Stacy Adams clothes, sweaters. When I grew up, I always had the basic shit. [My parents] were wealthy and I always got [cheap] shoes and shit and I was always in competition with other kids and [my parents] never understood that. So I would go out and buy me Nikes. I'd buy three brand new sixty-dollar pairs of shoes and clothes. (Joe Wilson—No. 099)

> A lot of times I'll buy clothes or tennis shoes or some jogging outfits, something like that. Some type of jacket or buy a hat. (Maurice Ross—No. 040)

Wearing appropriate clothing is an important aspect of fitting into any social situation. This is no less true for street culture, which has its own "dress code." As Anderson (1990) has observed, dressing in the latest status symbol clothing is virtually mandatory for those who want to be seen as hip on the street. The subjects in our sample were responding to this fact by using the money that they made from burglary to purchase fashionable outfits.

After clothes, cars and car accessories were the next most popular status items bought by the offenders. Seven of the 43 reported spending at least some of the money they got from burglaries on their cars.

> I spent [the money] on stuff for my car. Like I said, I put a lot of money into my car . . . I had a '79 Grand Prix, you know, a nice car. (Matt Detteman — No. 072)

The attributes of a high-status vehicle varied. Not all of these offenders, for example, would have regarded a 1979 Grand Prix as conferring much prestige on its owner. Nevertheless, they were agreed that driving a fancy or customized car, like wearing fashionable clothing, was an effective way of enhancing one's street status.

A sizable portion of the offenders therefore used the profits from their offenses to acquire the material trappings of success. In doing so, they sought to create an impression of affluence and hipness so that they would be admired by their peers on the street and by others. A British burglar interviewed by Bennett and Wright (1984:139) made explicit reference to the desire of offenders to be seen as a "better class of person."

> I don't know if you've ever thought about it, but I think every crook likes the life of thieving and then going and being somebody better. Really, you are deceiving people; letting them think that you are well off . . . You've got a nice car, you can go about and do this and do that. It takes money to buy that kind of life.

Shover and Honaker (1990:11) have suggested that the concern of offenders with outward appearances, as with their notorious high-living, grows out of what is typically a strong attachment to the values of street culture; values which place great emphasis on the "ostentatious enjoyment and display of luxury items." In a related vein, Katz (1988) has argued that for those who are committed to streetlife, the reckless spending of cash on luxury goods is an end in itself, demonstrating their disdain for the ordinary citizen's pursuit of financial security. Seen through the eyes of the offenders, therefore, money spent on such goods has not been "blown," but rather represents a cost of raising or maintaining one's status on the street.

Keeping Things Together

While most of the offenders spent much of the money they earned through residential burglary on drugs and clothes, a substantial number also used some of it for daily living expenses. Of the 95 who committed burglaries to raise money, 50 claimed that they needed the cash for subsistence.

> I do [burglaries] to keep myself together, keep myself up. (James Brown—No. 025)

Necessities mentioned most frequently were food, shelter, and clothing for the children. Thirty-eight of the 50 offenders (76 percent) reported using money from their burglaries to pay for one or all of these needs. Some of them used the money *solely* for such expenses.

> [I spend the money from my burglaries for] needs, not wants, needs—roof over my head, food in my mouth and things for my kids. (Lynn—No. 095)

The majority, however, paid for their immediate subsistence needs and spent the remaining cash on status-enhancing items and high-living.

> [I use burglary money to buy] food, clothing, drugs—in that order. And a place to stay, that's gon come automatic cause I'm a always find a place to stay. (No. 035)

Quite a few of the offenders—13 of 50—said that they paid bills with the money derived from burglary. Here again, however, there is a danger of being misled by such claims. To be sure, these offenders did use some of their burglary money to take care of bills. Often, though, the bills were badly delinquent because the offenders avoided paying them for as long as possible — even when they had the cash — in favor of buying, most typically, drugs. It was not until the threat of serious repercussions created unbearable pressure for the offenders that they relented and settled their accounts.

> [Sometimes I commit burglaries when] things pressuring me, you know? I got to do somethin' about these bills. Bills. I might let it pass that mornin'. Then I start trippin' on it at night and, next thing you know, it's wakin' me up. Yeah, that's when I got to get out and go do a burglary. I *got* to pay this electric bill off, this gas bill, you know? (No. 009)

Similarly, several of the subjects in our sample reported doing burglaries to pay parking or traffic tickets they had long ignored, having preferred to use their money for high-living.

> I started getting tickets and it was, like, I got four tickets for improper registration plates. Then it was like, "Hey, I need some money, this stuff is calculating up." I [needed] some money and I [didn't] want to run and ask Mom. So I just did [a burglary]. (No. 010)

Spontaneity is a prominent feature of street culture (Shover and Honaker, 1992); it is not surprising that many of the offenders displayed a marked tendency to live for the moment. Often they would give every indication of intending to take care of their obligations, financial or otherwise, only to be distracted by more immediate temptations. For instance, a woman in our sample, after being paid for an interview, asked us to drive her to a place where she could buy a pizza for her children's lunch. On the way to the restaurant, however, she changed her mind and asked to be dropped off at a crack house instead. In another case, we persuaded a male subject to allow three consultants on our research to come along on a visit to the scene of his most recent residential burglary in exchange for a larger than usual participation fee. At the agreed time and place, we arrived to find him sitting with friends in a car in an incoherent state; he had used the promised research payment as a means of obtaining cocaine on credit and was in the process of consuming it despite his scheduled meeting with us!

Katz (1988:216) has suggested that, through irresponsible spending, persistent offenders seek to construct "an environment of pressures that guide[s] them back toward crime." Whether offenders spend money in a conscious attempt to create such pressures is arguable; the subjects in our sample gave no indication of doing so, appearing simply to be financially irresponsible. One offender, for example, told us that he never hesitated to spend money, adding, "Why should I? I can always get some more." However, the inclination of offenders to free-spending leaves them with few alternatives but to continue committing crimes. Their next financial crisis is never far around the corner.

The high-living of the offenders, thus, calls into question the extent to which they are driven to crime by genuine financial hardship. At the same time, though, their spendthrift ways ensure that the crimes they commit will be economically motivated (Katz, 1988). The offenders perceive themselves as needing money, and their offenses typically are a response to this perception. Objectively, however, few are doing burglaries to escape impoverishment.

Why Burglary?

The decision to commit a residential burglary, then, is usually prompted by a perceived need for cash. Burglary, however, is not the only means by which offenders could get some money. Why do they choose burglary over legitimate work? Why do they elect to carry out a burglary rather than borrow the money from a friend or relative? Additionally, why do they select burglary rather than some other crime?

Given the streetcorner context in which most burglary decisions were made, legitimate work did not represent a viable solution for most of the offenders in our sample. These subjects, with few exceptions, wanted money there and then and, in such circumstances, even day labor was irrelevant because it did not respond to the immediacy of their desire for cash (Lemert, 1953). Moreover, the jobs available to most of the offenders were poorly-paid and could not sustain their desired lifestyles. It is notable that 17 of the 95 offenders who did burglaries primarily to raise money *were* legitimately employed.

> [I have a job, but] I got tired of waiting on that money. I can get money like that. I got talent, I can do me a burg, man, and get me five or six hundred dollars in less than a hour. Working eight hours a day and waiting for a whole week for a check and it ain't even about shit. (No. 022)

> [E]ven if I had a job, I betcha I couldn't find a job payin' me over minimum wage. Then they probably want to pay me every two weeks, so I would have to supplement that week that I wouldn't get paid with somethin'. (Mike Jackson—No. 046)

Beyond this, a few of the offenders expressed a strong aversion to legitimate employment, saying that a job would impinge upon their way of life.

> I ain't workin' and too lazy to work and just all that. I like it to where I can just run around. I don't got to get up at no certain time, just whenever I wake up. I ain't gotta go to bed a certain time to get up at a certain time. Go to bed around one o'clock or when I want, get up when I want. Ain't got to go to work and work eight hours. Just go in and do a five minute job, get that money, that's just basically it. (Tony Scott—No. 085)

> I done got lazy . . . I don't even want to work eight hours. I figure I can do maybe only one hour and get paid as much as I would if I worked a full day. (Kip Harris—No. 069)

These subjects closely matched the "high-level thieves" described by Shover (1991:92): "Misfits in a world that values precise schedules, punctuality, and disciplined subordination to authority, high-level thieves value the autonomy to structure life and work as they wish." Indeed, crime appealed to some of the subjects precisely because it allowed them to flaunt their independence from the routine imposed by the world of work (Shover and Honaker, 1992). Not taking orders from anyone—be it a girlfriend, a wife, or an employer—is a bedrock value on which male streetcorner culture rests; to be regarded as hip one must always do as he pleases. Accordingly, those who defined themselves most strongly in terms of their street reputation found the idea of getting a job to be distasteful because legitimate employment would require them to do as they were told by the boss.

> I guess [burglary is] in my blood. I don't too much want to work with a job and listen to no boss. But I can, like, do two or three burglaries and take money home to my kids. (Roger Brown—No. 058)

Nevertheless, a majority of the offenders reported that they wanted lawful employment; 43 of the 78 unemployed subjects who said that they did burglaries mostly for the money claimed they would stop committing offenses if someone gave them a "good" job.

> I'm definitely going to give it up as soon as I get me a good job. I don't mean making fifteen dollars an hour. Give me a job making five-fifty and I'm happy with it. I don't got to burglarize no more. I'm not doing it because I like doing it, I'm doing it because I need some [drugs]. (No. 079)

> Anything like five dollars an hour might slow me down, stop me completely. And the people at the job ain't buggin' me. I'll stay there the rest of my life if the people don't bother me cause I don't take nothing from 'em and therefore I would've went off on one of 'em or either beat 'em up. They don't bother me and I won't bother them and that five dollars is standin' strong. And wouldn't have to steal nothin' cause I'd have my money there. And I might cut down off my drugs—mainly you do drugs cause there's nothing to do. (No. 009)

(49)

While such claims may or may not be sincere—some of these subjects had held reasonably high-paying jobs in the past, but lost them owing to dishonesty or drug and alcohol problems— it is unlikely that they will ever be challenged. Decent employment opportunities are limited for inner-city residents (Wilson, 1987) and the offenders, who by and large are poorly educated, unskilled, and heavy illicit drug or alcohol users, are not well placed to compete for the few good jobs available. Most of them realized this and were resigned to being out of work. In their eyes, burglary represented a more realistic means of "earning" some money.

> Look, [there] ain't no job! I been out here lookin' for work, can't find no work. So I do what I do best. (Leroy Robison—No. 045)

Instead of committing burglaries, of course, the offenders perhaps could have borrowed some cash from a friend or relative. But they did not view this as a feasible alternative. Some of them were unwilling to ask for money because they felt that this would damage their status.

> I like to stand on my own two feet as a man, you know what I'm sayin'? I like to pay my way and I don't like to ask nobody for nothin'. Don't want nobody talkin' about me like I won't pay my way. I ain't freeloadin' off nobody. I'm a man, so I take care of myself. (Jeffery Moore—No. 006)

Others had borrowed money in the past, but were reluctant to ask for more.

> I can't keep askin' my wife, my brothers and sister and my mother. They'll tell me the same thing, "You a grown man, go out there and get you a job!" Or [they'll hand me some money and say], "Here, don't come back too soon." You know, you can only do that for so long. (No. 018)

And still others simply found that it was impossible to borrow money.

After you ask for a few dollars from people — your loved ones or your grandmother — and they tell you what they ain't got, you lay back down and try to go to sleep. You don't have no cigarettes, no beer, no nothing. Yeah, it builds up, animosity builds up inside you. Seems like that old devil just push you on out the door [to do a burglary]. (No. 069)

In any case, borrowing money offers only a short-term solution to financial needs. There usually is an expectation that loans will be repaid and this can provide the impetus for carrying out a burglary. Indeed, Katz (1988:217) has gone so far as to suggest that this obligation is a major source of the monetary troubles that drive offenders to crime: "Economic pressures toward crime emerge, not as the direct result of particular substantive needs as much as through the pressure of obligations accumulated in social networks. Borrowing and credit relations among offenders form a subtle, elaborate institution." In the course of our interviews we were told of burglaries that had been carried out because the offender owed money or wanted to reclaim a pawned article. We even encountered an offender who recently had broken into the residence of a fellow burglar in order to collect on a bad debt.

When faced with an immediate need for cash, then, the offenders in our sample perceived themselves as having little hope of getting money both quickly *and* legally. Many of the most efficient solutions to financial troubles are against the law (Lofland, 1969). However, this does not explain why the subjects decided specifically on the crime of residential burglary. After all, most of them admitted committing other sorts of offenses in the past, and some still were doing so. Why should they choose burglary?

For some subjects, this question held little relevance because they regarded residential burglary as their "main line" and alternative offenses were seldom considered when the need for money arose.

I guess the reason why I stick to burglary is because it makes me a lot of money . . . I guess you could say why I just do [burglary] is because I've been doing it for a while and I'm kind of stuck with it. (Carl Watson—No. 032)

[I do burglary] because it's easy and because I know it. It's kind of getting a speciality or a career. If you're in one line, or one field, and you know it real well, then you don't have any qualms about doing it. But if you try something new, you could really mess up . . . At this point, I've gotten away with so much [that] I just don't want to risk it—it's too much to risk at this point. I feel like I have a good pattern, clean; go in the house, come back out, under two minutes every time. (Darlene White—No. 100)

[Burglary is] easy for me. People have armed robberies and sell crack or whatever; I do burglaries. That's the easiest thing I do . . . I'm just saying that's what best suits me. (Karl Alverez—No. 081)

I don't know [why I decided on burglary]. I guess I'm good at it . . . I just like burglary, that's it. (No. 013)

When these subjects did commit another kind of offense, it typically was triggered by the chance discovery of a vulnerable target. As noted in the first chapter, most of the burglars we interviewed identified themselves as hustlers, people who were always looking to "get over" by making some fast cash; it would have been out of character for them to pass up any kind of presented opportunity to do so.

If I see another hustle, then I'll do it, but burglary is my pet. (Larry Smith—No. 065)

Burglars usually just stick to burglary. There's only one time that I was in the process of doing a burglary and I did a robbery. I was gettin' ready to do a burglary and a guy walked up and had a money sack. So I forgot all about the burglary and got the money sack. (No. 055)

The immediacy of their need for money, however, drove most of the offenders to look actively for any illicit opportunity to obtain cash rapidly, and they were open to crimes other than residential burglary. As one put it: "When you need money, you're going to do what you have to." These offenders chose to break into a dwelling when that act represented what they perceived to be the "most proximate and performable" (Lofland, 1969:61) crime available to them. Both their subjective state and the objective characteristics of the situation played a part in shaping this perception. For such offenders, making the decision to commit a residential burglary instead of another type of offense involved more than a cool assessment of the potential costs and benefits associated with the various alternatives; emotion, mood, and intuition also had a powerful influence on this process (Scheff, 1992).

> [S]ometimes you feel better about one thing than you do another and sometimes you know where the money is at. It depends on what's there at the time, whether there is transportation or you are in the area. It's just what looks good at the time. What's more comfortable for you to do, what feels better. (Earl Martin—No. 083)

> [W]hen you high on crack, you want some more crack and you don't want to wait, so you got to do a robbery. Now a burglary, you might be high at three in the morning, now whose house can you go in at three in the morning and they ain't gonna be there? (Diamond Craig—No. 027)

A few offenders typically did not themselves choose to commit residential burglaries, but went along with offenses suggested by someone else. In need of cash, these subjects were especially receptive to presented criminal opportunities, even if they were not particularly enamored of burglary.

> I got a friend that do burglaries with me. He usually the one that sets them up. If he ain't got one set up, then I might go off into somethin' else. (Larry Brown—No. 052)

Some of these offenders seemed, when on their own, to lack the stomach for any sort of serious wrongdoing. Others had a preference for a different type of crime, but were tempted to do an occasional burglary when asked to lend a hand. One subject told us that he usually stayed away from burglary in favor of drug selling, explaining that he regarded the former as morally worse than the latter because "the victim comes to you in drug selling, [while] in burglary you go to the victim." Nevertheless, he admitted being willing to commit a break-in when presented with a good opportunity by one of his associates.

The range of moneymaking crimes from which the majority of the offenders could choose was fairly limited. By and large, they did not hold jobs that would allow them to violate even a low-level position of financial trust (Cressey, 1953). Similarly, few had the technical expertise required to disarm the sophisticated security systems protecting lucrative commercial targets or the interpersonal skills needed to commit frauds. It is not surprising, therefore, that, besides residential burglary, almost all of them stuck to a limited number of crimes requiring little skill, such as theft (mostly shoplifting), stealing cars, streetcorner drug selling and robbery.

For many of the offenders, the few profitable criminal opportunities objectively available to them were restricted still further by their belief that certain crimes were too risky or were morally unacceptable. A number of them, for instance, had curtailed or severely limited their participation in drug selling because they felt that the risks of apprehension and punishment were too great.

> It's hard right now, man . . . I can go back to selling drugs
> which I could lose my ass. A burg, I could get away with
> four years [imprisonment]. If I get caught on burglary, I
> know I'm guaranteed four years. I get caught with drugs, I'm
> a do thirty [years]. So see, I got away from drugs and fell with
> the number one [offense, burglary]. (Charlie – No. 024)

> See, right now they harder on druggies than a burglar or auto
> thief. They tryin' to save the younger generation now. They
> sayin' drugs is the cause of the crimes now. (Joe Outlaw –
> No. 056)

Likewise, some regarded robbery, especially armed robbery, as carrying too much risk.

> See, if you rob a person, they can identify you cause you lookin' right at 'em, you know? They lookin' right at you and they can identify you. And armed robbery is what? Five to ten [years]? Or ten to fifteen [years]? (No. 006)

> [T]hey givin' too much time for robbin'. After my eight years for robbery, I told myself then I'll never do another robbery because I was locked up with so many guys that was doin' twenty-five to thirty years for robbery and I think that's what made me stick to burglaries, because I had learned that a crime committed with a weapon will get you a lot of time. (No. 013)

One offender decided against committing robberies because he was afraid of being hurt by the victim or witnesses.

> I'm not going to try no strong robberies cause these people could possibly see me out there in the street and I might be full of some alcohol or something and they could get me. They could shoot me or stab me or anything and I wouldn't know. (No. 040)

A couple of the burglars we worked with believed that it was wrong to threaten or to use violence to get money and therefore were reluctant to do robberies. Although the offender quoted below does not say that he avoided robbery for moral reasons, the tone of his voice left no doubt that this was the case.

> I'd never personally rob a human being, like walk up to them and say, "Give me you wallet and give me your purse!" No way. (No. 079)

Even those who were willing to do robberies, however, sometimes were unable to do so because they did not have the "facilitating hardware" (Lofland, 1969:69–72), namely, a firearm.

Well, lately I haven't did any [robberies]. But when I was doin' it, I robbed every Friday . . . I ain't got no pistol, that's the only reason [I haven't been doing them], . . . I swear. (No. 011)

Handguns are in great demand on the street. One of the subjects in our sample claimed that he would rather have a pistol than cash because "a gun is money with a trigger." Offenders who are in need of immediate cash often are tempted to sell their weapon instead of resorting to a difficult or risky crime. The result of this is that they do not always have a pistol at their disposal. In such circumstances residential burglary, which typically requires nothing more than readily available objects (e.g., a screwdriver, hammer, or small crowbar) for its commission, becomes correspondingly more attractive.

The Seductions of Residential Burglary

For some offenders, the perceived benefits of residential burglary may transcend the amelioration of financial need. A few of the subjects we interviewed — 7 of 102 — said that they did not typically commit burglaries as much for the money as for the psychic rewards. These offenders reported breaking into dwellings primarily because they enjoyed doing so. Most of them did not enjoy burglary per se, but rather the risks and challenges inherent in the crime.

[I]t's really because I like [burglaries]. I know that if I get caught I'm a do more time than the average person, but still, it's the risk. I like doin' them. (No. 013)

I think [burglary is] fun. It's a challenge. You don't know whether you're getting caught or not and I like challenges. If I can get a challenging [burglary, I] like that. It's more of the risk that you got to take, you know, to see how good you can really be. (No. 103)

These subjects seemingly viewed the successful completion of an offense as "a thrilling demonstration of personal competence" (Katz, 1988:9). Given this, it is not surprising that the catalyst for their crimes often was a mixture of boredom and an acute sense of frustration born of failure at legitimate activities such as work or school.

> [Burglary] just be something to do. I might not be workin' or not going to school – not doing anything. So I just decide to do a burglary. (No. 017)

The offense provided these offenders with more than something exciting to do; it also offered them the chance to "be somebody" by successfully completing a dangerous act. Similarly, Shover and Honaker (1992:288) have noted that, through crime, offenders seek to demonstrate a sense of control or mastery over their lives and thereby to gain "a measure of respect, if not from others, at least from [themselves]."

The purest example of the psychic rewards of residential burglary was provided by a probationer who, because he denied being currently active, was not included in our sample. Nevertheless, we spoke to him at great length. This man described, with obvious glee, breaking in to places, rearranging the furniture and leaving, often without taking anything. He portrayed himself as a prankster, explaining that he got a great charge out of picturing the victims trying to make a credible-sounding police report. That his motivations were more sinister, however, was suggested when he commented: "I know that [the victims] are still wondering what I took. And I didn't take a thing!" Though the offenses had occurred months earlier, this individual still appeared to derive satisfaction from having desecrated the living space of his victims; he clearly was pleased by the prospect that his actions continued to unsettle their lives. Katz (1988:69) noted a phenomenon closely akin to this among the offenders he surveyed, concluding that nonacquisitive burglaries were experienced as a "black sacrament," a quasi-religious act of defilement through which criminals attempted "to project something negative into the victim's world."

While only a small number of the subjects in our sample

said that they were motivated *primarily* by the psychic rewards of burglary, many of them perceived such rewards as a
secondary benefit of the offense. Sixteen of the 95 offenders
who did burglaries to raise cash also said that they found the
crime to be "exciting" or "thrilling."

> Burglary is excitin'. [I do it] mostly for the money, but a lot
> of times it arouses my suspicion and curiosity. (No. 046)

> [Beyond money], it's the thrill. If you get out [of the house],
> you smile and stand on it, breathe out. (No. 045)

> It's just a thrill going in undetected and walking out with all
> they shit. Man, that shit fucks me up. (No. 022)

Several of those who were motivated predominantly by financial pressures claimed that the offense represented "a challenge" or "an adventure" as well.

> It wasn't just gettin' money . . . it was just the thing of doing
> it, the thrill out of going in [the house] and doing it. I guess
> it was a challenge. (No. 055)

> [Burglary] is a challenge . . . like going on a treasure hunt.
> (Billy Kelly—No. 048)

> [After the money, burglary] is adventure to me. (Rodney
> Price—No. 057)

And a number of the subjects who reported committing burglaries mostly as a way of making money added that breaking
into dwellings was "fun" too.

> [I do burglaries] for the money. Sometimes it is kind of fun.
> (Ed Alverez—No. 082)

Finally, one of the offenders who did burglaries chiefly for
monetary reasons alluded to the fact that the crime also provided him with a valued identity.

Deciding to Commit a Burglary

My main reason [for committing burglaries] is because of
the money . . . and knowin' that you can hustle, knowin'
that you a hustler. (No. 054)

Beyond all of this, quite a few of the offenders who *usually*
resorted to burglary out of financial need occasionally committed the offense to get even with someone for a real or imagined wrong. A number of them mentioned doing burglaries
from time to time for "revenge." In the case below, for example, a black offender broke into the home of a young white
man who had called him "a nigger" during an altercation over
a scratched car door.

I was driving my mother's car and [I pulled into the parking
lot of a convenience store]. When I opened my door, I hit
this guy's car — a gray Cutlass — and he wanted to fight about
it . . . So we were going to [settle it there], but the police
broke it up. So I was thinking about gettin' even . . . I followed him [home] . . . I just kept him in sight till I seen what
house he was staying in . . . It was Wednesday and, uh, I was
plannin' on doing it Friday, but I had to learn their routine
first. I watched a little bit the rest of Wednesday and then I
came back and watched it a little bit Thursday, but, uh, I
had to move quick cause I wanted to get even . . . That was
a grudge there, a pay back, so it wasn't too much for the
money. I broke up more stuff in there than I stole . . . Normally when I break in a house, it's so that I can get me a
high, cause I be having the urge to smoke a little coke. But
this particular day, they just pissed me off. I just wanted to
get even. I just wanted to hit 'em where it hurts — in they
pocket — and I think I did pretty good. (John Black — No. 008)

Other offenders described break-ins designed to punish an ex-
lover, collect on a bad debt, or "pay back" an unscrupulous
drug dealer. Black (1983:34) has suggested that crimes such
as these are essentially moralistic and involve "the pursuit of
justice." Indeed, he has gone so far as to argue that many burglaries are best thought of as a form of self-help or "secret so-

cial control" (Black, 1983:37). This may be overstating the matter, but it is clear that, on occasion, some offenders find burglary an appealing means of righting a perceived wrong. For instance, several burglars in our sample who often worked together reported targeting the homes of homosexuals who were buying up and renovating property on the periphery of their own neighborhood. These offenders explained that they did not like gays and broke into their dwellings as a means of forcing them to move out of the area. From their perspective, such crimes were justifiable in the circumstances; they represented an attempt to keep the neighborhood from being overrun by outsiders whose way of life was different and threatening.

Summary

Offenders typically decided to commit a residential burglary in response to a perceived need. In most cases, this need was financial, calling for the immediate acquisition of money. However, it sometimes involved what was interpreted as a need to repel an attack on the status, identity, or self-esteem of the offenders. Whatever its character, the need almost invariably was regarded by the offenders as pressing, that is, as something that had to be dealt with immediately. Lofland (1969:50) has observed that most people, when under pressure, have a tendency to become fixated on removing the perceived cause of that pressure "as quickly as possible." Those in our sample were no exception. In such a state, the offenders were not predisposed to consider unfamiliar, complicated, or long-term solutions (see Lofland, 1969:50–54) and instead fell back on residential burglary, which they knew well. This often seemed to happen almost automatically, the crime occurring with minimal calculation as part of a more general path of action (e.g., partying). To the extent that the offense ameliorated their distress, it nurtured a tendency for them to view burglary as a reliable means of dealing with similar pressures in the future. In this way, a foundation was laid for the continuation of their present lifestyle which, by and large, revolved around the street culture. The self-indulgent activities sup-ported by this culture, in turn, precipitated new pressures; and thus a vicious cycle developed.

That the offenders, at the time of actually contemplating offenses, typically perceived themselves to be in a situation of immediate need has at least two important implications. First, it suggests a mind-set in which they were seeking less to maxi-mize their gains than to deal with a present crisis. Second, it indicates an element of desperation which might have weak-ened the influence of threatened sanctions and neutralized any misgivings about the morality of breaking into dwellings (see Shover and Honaker, 1992). We will return to these issues at various points throughout the book.

3 *Choosing the Target*

THE MOTIVATION TO COMMIT a residential burglary is not itself sufficient to cause offenders to carry out the offense. Obviously, they must pick out a specific dwelling before acting on that motivation. In theory, the supply of residential properties is so vast that finding a target would seem to be a simple matter. In practice, however, potential targets are fairly limited. The offenders, after all, typically are seeking to solve a pressing problem, financial or other, and feel under pressure to act quickly. At the same time, they are reluctant to break in to a place without first determining the potential risks and rewards. As offenders attempt to settle on a target, therefore, they are under the influence of two seemingly conflicting demands: one calling for immediate action, and the other counselling caution. How do they manage to reconcile these demands and select a specific dwelling? That is the question which this chapter seeks to answer. This issue already has received considerable attention from researchers, especially from those favoring a rational choice explanation of property offending (e.g., Bennett and Wright, 1984; Cromwell et al., 1991). These researchers, however, have failed to place the target selection process into the wider context of the lifestyles and daily activities of offenders.

It is widely assumed that offenders typically make a decision to commit a residential burglary and only then set out to search for a suitable target. Burglary prevention advice admonishing homeowners to create the illusion of occupancy while they are away—by, among other things, using an automatic timer to switch lights on and off—clearly is founded on this assumption. A great deal of the experimental research on the way in which burglars choose targets also rests on the same paradigm (e.g., Bennett and Wright, 1983; 1984; Logie et al., 1992; Nee and Taylor, 1988; Taylor and Nee, 1988; Wright and Logie, 1988). In reality, offenders often have a potential target in mind when they decide to do a burglary and, therefore, have no need to search for one. Nearly nine out of ten of the subjects in our sample—89 of 100—said that usually they had decided on a specific dwelling *before* setting out to commit the burglary. These subjects were unwilling to break into a residence without knowing something about the people who lived there and the kinds of things it contained.

> I never go into a house where I don't know nothing about it or who's [living] there. You got to at least know something. (Andre Neal—No. 059)

Accordingly, when the need for money arose, they would not simply search for a target and commit a spur-of-the-moment offense; they had to have a place already lined up, that is, they needed reliable information regarding its contents and the routine of the residents. In practice, this could be accomplished in one of three ways: (1) through knowing the occupants; (2) through receiving a tip; or (3) through observing a potential target.

Chapter 3

Knowing the Occupants

It is taken for granted among criminologists that crimes of violence often involve a victim who is known to the offender. Research on homicide (e.g., Wolfgang, 1958), rape (e.g., Amir, 1971), and assault (e.g., Vera Institute, 1977) consistently has shown this to be the case. Less well appreciated is the fact that the offender knows the victim in a sizable proportion of certain property crimes (Black, 1983). Shover (1991:93), based on an examination of National Crime Survey data, concluded that "upward of 42 percent of victims who chance to encounter a burglar in their home may discover the burglar is not a stranger." More than one in five of the offenders we interviewed — 21 of 100 — reported that typically they chose to break into dwellings where they knew the occupants.

> [N]ine times out of ten, if I am just laying around the house with nothing to do [and] I want some fast money, I just try to [choose a target using] the people I know and got their phone numbers. "Where you going? What you up to? You gonna leave? Who's at the house now?" . . . I can find out where they be at. (No. 069)

Only a few offenders selected targets belonging to relatives or close friends. Most picked homes occupied by what might be termed casual acquaintances, who often were neighborhood residents encountered by the offenders in the course of their daily rounds (see Walsh, 1986).

> I knew [the burglary victim] before anyway. We was all just on the street getting high and drinking. [The victim] said, "We can go to my house and smoke this shit." That's how I ended up over at his house . . . He wasn't a friend of mine, just somebody I knew. I was at their house getting high and it was, like, three days later I wanted to get high [again] and I needed some money. I was thinking, "Where can I make some money at?" I said, "I can go over to John's house." (No. 079)

In many cases, the offenders had not become acquainted with the victims in order to burglarize their dwellings. Rather, they tended to select these places on short notice, typically because they wanted money quickly and knew there was something inside worth stealing. Often these decisions resulted from a session of spontaneous partying, with offenders being invited to visit the home of a would-be victim for the purpose of socializing and then noticing something of value. One subject explained the process this way: "Like, say I be over at your house and you might have a motherfucking solid gold lamp on the table. Now I ain't saying that I plan to steal it from you, but we over there. Then tomorrow I wake up and I need some money; I can get about forty dollars for that motherfucker." In such circumstances, the offenders seldom reported selecting their targets by carefully weighing up a variety of possible places to attack; instead, the idea of burglarizing one particular dwelling suddenly popped into their heads as they contemplated ways to get some fast cash.

Quite a few of the offenders targeted residences belonging to acquaintances whom they knew to be drug dealers. In doing a dealer's place, they were able to obtain drugs directly and avoid the problem of converting stolen goods into cash.

> I knew exactly where to go to get what I needed. I didn't want no items. I didn't want to have to sell nothing. I just wanted to get some drugs and some money, so I knew exactly where to go. (No. 069)

These offenses could be carried out more or less on the spur of the moment precisely because the offenders were acquainted with the victims and, at a minimum, knew something about their daily movements. An added benefit of burglarizing dwellings belonging to drug dealers, of course, was that such people were unlikely to report break-ins to the police.

A number of the offenders in our sample cultivated relationships with people with the express purpose of burglarizing their residences. One female offender, for instance, regularly picked up men in bars as a means of locating potential burglary sites. She would strike up a conversation with a man drinking alone, spend the evening in his company surreptitiously gathering information about such things as his work and travel schedule, and eventually agree to accompany him to his place for sex. While at this residence, she would check for any special security devices, note the floor plan, and determine the location of valuables—a task that she found easy: "You know how men are, they always want to show off. So they get out their gun collection or coin collection, stamp collection or whatever. They always do." Several weeks later she would return, often with her boyfriend, to break into the dwelling. Similarly, two other female offenders, working as partners, usually located targets in the course of their prostitution activities. Advertising themselves as "two women for the price of one," they offered their clients, who often were intoxicated elderly men, an in-home service. Once inside a residence, one of the women would distract the man while the other would steal his keys. After two or three days had passed, they would come back and do the burglary. Likewise, one of the male subjects worked hard to establish rapport with local drug dealers so that he could set them up for a burglary.

> My house burglaries are based on dope dealers. The way I do it is watch them, learn them, get up under them—try to get next to them and peep [the house] to find out where the stash is at. I might not hit them that day, or that time, or that month; not until I've learned it. (No. 024)

Other offenders did not go to such lengths to get to know their victims beforehand, but rather identified potential targets during conversations with people they met. Always on the lookout for burglary sites, these offenders casually asked those they encountered about where they lived, who lived with them, their vacation plans, and so on. A number of the subjects claimed, not always convincingly, that they had a special gift which allowed them to extract this information from intended victims without arousing their suspicion.

I got a magical way about me. I pat myself on the back, it is a magic. The average person tell me that they see a halo over my head. Nobody knows I do anything wrong; it is a magical feeling. See, I know how to strike up a conversation with you. I know how to talk to you that would make you have confidence in me. (Running Wolf Woods—No. 036)

Offenders who had jobs that gave them the chance to enter people's homes legitimately found it particularly easy to locate prospective burglary targets. Several, for instance, were employed by home decorating or remodeling companies. These offenders frequently spent days or weeks working in the same residence; this allowed them to get a good sense of the occupants' daily routine. What is more, they often were left unsupervised by homeowners. This provided ample opportunities to explore dwellings unmolested, checking security arrangements, and determining where valuables were kept.

In my everyday routine, I can see things. Like, I works for a interior decorator company, so I travels a lot and I sees a lot . . . When [the company] calls me . . . to go set up paneling or something, I look around. [The occupants] got money; they buyin' from that company, they got some money. (Bob More—No. 012)

Other subjects we interviewed were employed as cable television installers, movers, or delivery persons. While none of these jobs allowed offenders to spend long in any given residence, they gave them a chance to see how a place was furnished, how well protected it was, and how it was laid out.

I went in [the house] to work, to install cable . . . [and] the first thing I seen was this chandelier sittin' up in the living room and, like I say, I been doing burglaries and messin' with crystal and jewelry so much that I knew that was an expensive chandelier. The person that was lettin' me in to install the cable had about three rings on they finger . . . and I know the difference between [fake] and real diamonds. Fake stones and fake gold, I know the difference . . . So that made up my mind [to commit the burglary] right then. When I put the cable in, I seen how easy it was to get in; they had a patio door with no security system on it. (No. 056)

Moreover, occupants often unwittingly offered extra information to these offenders, casually discussing, for example, an upcoming vacation or business trip.

When I was reconnecting the cable line, I overheard the lady talking on the phone and saying they be out of town for a few days. And when I heard that, I knew what time it was, time to come back and help them out; watch they house for them. (No. 056)

Offenders who worked on the outside of residences (e.g., roofers or gardeners) also could gather information about potential targets. At a minimum, they could watch occupants come and go and develop some notion of their daily schedule without attracting suspicion. They often were permitted to enter dwellings to get a drink of water, make a telephone call, or use the toilet, and thereby were able to learn a good deal more about the interior. One study subject, a gardener, was given a house key by the owners of a residence so that he could let himself in when they were not at home. He worked for these people for some time and did not steal anything from them as long as he remained in their employ. Shortly before quitting, he had a duplicate key cut. He continues to use this key to gain entry to the house from time to time, despite the fact that the residence has changed hands twice. On each occasion, he is careful to steal just one small item, believing that with no sign of a forced entry the occupants either will not miss the piece or will conclude that they have misplaced it. As he put it: "See, they not expectin' it. If you go takin', like a TV or stereo and stuff like that, that's easy to miss. But by the time they find out that I done took somethin', I'm back again and done got somethin' else." He noted that a major advantage of burglarizing the same place repeatedly was that one developed a fairly reliable way of predicting when the occupants would be away.

> I always go back [to the same places] because, once you been there, you know just about when you been there before and when you can go back. And every time I hit a house, it's always on the same day [of the week] I done been before cause I know there ain't nobody there. (John Ross—No. 051)

This might go some way toward explaining the general process by which certain dwellings come to be burglarized repeatedly (Forrester et al., 1988). People are creatures of routine; having established through offending that the residents of an attractive target were out at a given time of day burglars can be fairly confident that the dwelling will usually be unoccupied at this time. Why, then, should they select a brand new target where the presence of occupants may be more at issue?

Several unemployed offenders, aware that certain jobs offered opportunities to collect useful information about possible burglary targets without arousing undue suspicion, disguised themselves as door-to-door salespersons. Carrying a clipboard, they would canvas a neighborhood claiming to represent, say, a home remodeling company. When homeowners expressed an interest in having some work done, the offenders would ask about their schedule so that "a convenient time for an estimate can be arranged." They also requested a telephone number "just in case our estimator is delayed." Using such tactics, the offenders often were able to get all of the information they needed to determine when the occupants of a potential target were in and out. And sometimes they learned considerably more. One subject, for instance, occasionally adopted the ruse of being a salesperson for an alarm company and, in this way, learned about existing security arrangements.

A few of the offenders admitted that they sometimes targeted the homes of people they knew well. Such crimes usually were directed against people the offenders did not like or had fallen out with, such as a former associate or girlfriend, and thus were not morally problematic for them. Moreover, selecting a dwelling they were intimately familiar with made the offense less risky.

> A guy was delivering some [cocaine] for me and I knew he lived by himself and I knew where everything was in his house and I knew exactly what he had. And I sat there and said, "Get rid of this [cocaine] for me." I gave him an ounce and a half. That's a lot of fucking money. And I knew everything he had in his house. He had a nice assortment of guns, that's where I got that M1 I told you about . . . I knew exactly where he was going and how long it would take him. He was a nerd; he looked funny and I didn't like him. He had a lot of shit . . . [so] I walk in, grab the shit and leave. (Chris Leisure—No. 031)

> [T]he reason I decided to do this one, well, me and my girlfriend fell out so, uh, I needed some money and I remembered the layout of this house. So I went through the side window on the back porch, uh, there's a screen window but, when you push it, it'll fall right in . . . So I went in and just ransacked the place . . . I knew what they had in the home . . . [and] I just knew their schedule, I knew their schedule down to a T. (No. 008)

Although it was rare for the offenders to break into dwellings occupied by relatives or those they regarded as close friends, such offenses were not unknown.

> I be knowin' what house I'm going to hit. It could be a friend of mine, I could be over at his house all last week, know he got a new VCR; we been lookin' at movies. I know what time they work. I know where his wife at or he stay by himself. (No. 079)

Indeed, one subject told us that he actually preferred doing places owned by relatives—"kin people"—because he was familiar with their daily routine. More commonly, though, the offenders found it distasteful to victimize those they were close to and resorted to doing so only when they felt particularly desperate. On these occasions, it was not unusual for them to experience pangs of conscience and to limit the amount stolen to what they regarded as their minimum requirement.

I was . . . high [on crack] . . . I needed some money, so I called [a friend] up and she said she wasn't going to give it to me and I knew that she was going to work. So when I knew that she was gone, I went in and busted the door in through the back. It was a four-family flat . . . [A]fter I got in, I said I wasn't going to hurt her real bad so I'll just take a little bit. (No. 025)

[A friend of mine] told me she was leavin', goin' out of town. And I knew some of the things she had in her house cause I been in there. I didn't have no money, didn't have no beer, and that's a no-no . . . I was sittin' there and I was thinkin', "Where can I get me some money?" and I usually tries not to think about people I know. [Anyway] I was sayin' I'm sorry as I went in. I apologized as I was goin' in: "Baby, I'm sorry, I don't mean to do this, but, hey, better you than me." (No. 012)

It is interesting that while the relatives and good friends of offenders were insulated to some degree from being victimized by them, this immunity did not seem to extend to the relatives and friends of good friends. Some of the subjects in our sample, for instance, recounted offenses in which they attacked homes belonging to parents of friends.

I have a band, but we practice over by my old singer's house. There's a big subdivision in the back. There are, not really farmhouses, but kind of boony houses that are nice. So I knew this girl that used to live there, but she moved away and her parents still lived there . . . That's the one I did because I knew how to get into it . . . They have a basement and a two story house. In the basement, there was the VCR and stuff so I just basically went in there . . . It was like [the girl] didn't live there anymore and I know her house pretty well, so I went to her house. (No. 081)

Others reported breaking in to the residences of friends of friends or relatives.

I was with this dude. He went to these people's house and he took me with him . . . Just visiting, you know, the people didn't know me and I didn't know them either. I just knew the dude that knew the people. So we went in [and we were just sitting around] and I unlocked the window. [No one knew] that I unlocked the window. There wasn't nobody in the room when I did it, so I just unlocked the window and went and sat in the living room by myself. That next morning I woke up, after I had thought about it all night, and I decided that I was gonna go get 'em. So I just woke up, went to they house, raised the window up and didn't have to break nothing. I just went in. (No. 011)

See, I got cousins stayin' [in a nearby neighborhood] and she has friends that like to go out and have parties on Saturday. I knew that from the jump start, so I just went on over there . . . I knew they weren't going to be home that night. I had a friend drop me off over there about two times that night and I seen them comin' out of the house earlier. So I busted them about an hour after they had left. I figured they were going to be gone for a while anyway. (No. 048)

Obviously, the loyalty of the offenders to others in their social circle often was not absolute—cynics might even call it situational—and, at the best of times, embraced only those closest to them. For the most part, these were self-centered individuals without notably strong bonds to other human beings; their allegiances seemed forever to be shifting to suit their own ends.

The finding that a substantial number of the offenders in our sample typically knew the people whose homes they victimized suggests that property crimes may not be all that different from violent ones in terms of the relationship between offender and victim. While some might object that the offenders often had only a very superficial acquaintanceship with their victims, this is true for many violent crimes as well. The important point is that burglars were able to take advantage of a preexisting relationship with potential victims — however brief or casual — to gather intelligence about their daily activities, possessions, and household security. This facilitated the selection of a target when the need to commit the crime arose. As Lofland (1969:73) has observed: "Built-in vulnerabilities in the standing social arrangements of [o]thers" have a way of becoming particularly obvious at these times.

Receiving a Tip

Where burglary offenders do not select their victims on the basis of personal knowledge, they may rely on "inside" information provided by others as a means of locating targets. Sometimes they receive this information from "tipsters," that is, people who regularly pass on intelligence about good burglary opportunities for a fee or a cut of the take (Shover, 1973). At other times offenders pick up information more informally through friends or criminal associates. This information is valuable to offenders because, as Shover (1973) has noted, it can reduce the risks as well as enhance the rewards of residential burglary considerably. Getting good intelligence about lucrative targets on anything approaching a routine basis requires that offenders have access to a reliable network. Not many do. Just six of the subjects in our sample said that they usually selected their residential targets on the basis of a tip given to them by someone else. What is more, only two of these offenders regularly used information from persons who might be considered tipsters. One of them had an arrangement with an airport employee under which he received information about departing passengers with local addresses.

[It's summer and] a lot of people are goin' to Hawaii, France, and Rome and stuff like that. Paris. I'm a be [busy]. (Eric Thompson — No. 047)

The other offender employed a crack user — a "rock head" — to gather intelligence about the comings and goings of drug dealers operating out of crack houses.

I got a rock head. All I got to do is fix him up [with money] and he could feed me all the information I need . . . Give him about thirty dollars and he go down to the dope house and rock shit up and smoke it. But, at the same time, he listening to what's going on and shit. See what I'm saying? He cool with these people too. But he cooler with me. So he sit down there and gather up all the information and I have it verified just to make sure. I have him go back the next day and he'll say, "Y'all still gon go out and do that?" "Yeah, we got these flights leavin' in thirty minutes" and shit like that! Boom! [I'm in there]. (No. 022)

The remaining subjects who routinely relied on tips as a means of locating targets picked up their information from various sources on the street.

I know a lot of people and they know my game, so they put me up on certain people: "So and so's leavin' town next week." I don't like nobody in the house . . . Say, for instance, a friend of theirs might be going out of town and they want something out of the deal, they ain't doing it for nothing. They scared to go do it, so they tell [me] about it. (Robert Johnson — No. 067)

These offenders did not have a formal arrangement for obtaining information about potential burglary targets. Their interest in such information, however, was well-known on the street and people often offered them a "lick," that is, a promising burglary site, in exchange for some part of the proceeds.

While only a few of the offenders regularly used information from others to locate targets, many of them occasionally did so. One offender, for example, took us to a mansion that he recently had burglarized. This offense was triggered by information received from one of the victim's neighbors, a well-to-do businessman who provided the offender with tips from time to time.

> [I didn't] find this house exactly, I went out to do a cable job. So the person I did the cable job for, like I say, he ain't exactly what you call straight up, he just live in a good place . . . and he told me that [the next door neighbors] had certain things that he wanted, so we compromised. I got what I wanted and he got what he wanted . . . You know; this person called me [later] and told me that [his neighbors] will be back [from vacation] this week and, if I was gonna take care of my business, do it now. (No. 056)

Another offender told us about several lucrative residential burglaries that he had committed with the aid of an insurance agent. The agent, using the files of coworkers as well as his own, was able to identify properties containing insured valuables and to determine any special security precautions. Several other subjects recounted offenses where a person employed as a maid or gardener had let them know that the occupants of a house would not be home at a certain time.

Cromwell et al. (1991), among others, have called attention to the role of otherwise honest citizens in encouraging burglary through their willingness to buy stolen goods. By contrast, the more direct participation of seemingly upstanding people who feed information about prospective targets to burglars has largely been overlooked by researchers. Although far less common among ordinary citizens than the buying of stolen goods, such collusion is particularly worrying because it often involves the violation of a position of trust. Successful, high-level burglars often rely heavily on information from inside sources in planning their crimes (Shover, 1991).

There is a question, of course, about the wisdom of acting on tips provided by people who in many cases are passing on information about neighbors, clients, or employers (Bennett and Wright, 1984). How far can these people be trusted? Some offenders disregarded tips altogether for this very reason, while others took precautions to avoid being set up for an arrest by those who provided them with leads.

> I picks my own days [to actually commit the burglary]. I picks my own days for the simple reason, just in case it's a cross in it. [The person who gave me the tip] don't know what day I'm there . . . See, you tell them you're going on another date and go a different one, just in case. (No. 056)

As far back as two decades ago, the offenders interviewed by Shover were bemoaning the fact that the code of honor among burglars specifying that they not betray associates appeared to be breaking down.

> Another change which many of those interviewed mentioned spontaneously is the gradual erosion of "the Code" among thieves. All seem to agree that the "solid," ethical career criminal seems to be giving way to the "hustler," an alert opportunist who is primarily concerned only with personal — as opposed to collective — security . . . This has not, however, altered the strong lip service accorded the code. (Shover, 1973:512–13)

In our research, we uncovered little evidence to suggest that such a criminal code continues to operate; if indeed, it ever did. Few of the subjects we spoke to expressed strong feelings of loyalty to their colleagues and many stated that they did not trust them. The predominant sentiment among them was, "You have to look out for number one." These offenders did not even pay lip service to the importance of upholding any code of "honor among thieves." That is hardly surprising. Streetlife, with its emphasis on enjoyment of the moment, discourages the formation of close, long-lasting social ties. As noted earlier, most of the burglars in our sample conducted their affairs without regard for the feelings of others; when the chips were down even friends and associates were liable to be judged as fair game in any sort of moneymaking scheme.

In summary, while few of the offenders regularly relied on tips as a means of locating targets, many of them occasionally selected a dwelling on the basis of inside knowledge provided by someone else. The people who gave them this information might be thought of as "facilitating others" (Lofland, 1969:72–81) in at least two senses. First, in assuming that the offenders wanted this information, they reinforced their deviant identity as people who were willing to commit residential burglaries. Perhaps they even conveyed, however subtly, an *expectation* that the offenders should act on the information given to them. Second, and more directly, by identifying a specific target, they handed the offenders an opportunity that could be exploited in a time of need.

Watching the Target

While in many residential burglaries the offenders have inside knowledge about the occupants either through personal acquaintance or by way of a tip provided by someone else, this certainly does not characterize all—or even most—such crimes. Nonetheless, most targets do not appear to be chosen randomly or on the spur of the moment. Oftentimes offenders have been watching a specific dwelling for some time prior to breaking in to it. Indeed, the majority of the subjects in our sample—62 of 100—reported that this typically was the case for them.

> I get about two [houses] a month, somewhere in there. It all depends on how my money is. [Just] because I'm always lookin' out there [for a place], don't make me do it every time. But I be lookin'. Then, if I just happen to be in the vicinity again, I might say, "Damn, this is the house I'm gon' get." Then I might see that house two or three more times 'fore I make up my mind to go in it . . . I look at a house two or three times before I go in it . . . But the day I go in, I done made my mind up. (James Cook—No. 016)

If we going shopping, for instance, we'll pick a house; we'll
be just walking around and stuff and we pick a house . . .
You see, it's real simple and easy, you know. We watch it
for a while, we don't just go jump into it. It's got to be a
house we done watched for a while. (Sharon Adams –
No. 071)

Through observing residences, the offenders were able to acquire various bits and pieces of information about the occupants, the most important of which was their daily routine.
Almost all of the offenders who regularly watched potential
targets beforehand, said that they did so to "clock" the comings and goings of the residents.

I don't just go there and do a burglary. I done already checked
it out. I can sit back for about a month and estimate how
many people are there. What time they leave and what time
they coming back. Just like the police do; sitting in front of
a dope house and watching how many people are coming or
going out of there. (Mike Bird – No. 028)

Well, first you have to look at the house. You don't want to
go in when the people are there [so] you check it out a day
or two and see what they schedule is. See when they go to
work, when they get home, where the kids at. (No. 057)

You have to go out and look and see what's the best. What's
what and where [the occupants] gonna be, how long they
gonna be there. Does the wife work? Husband work? You
find them things out. You could see that early in the morning. If two cars are there and both of them are gone between
eight and twelve, then you know both of them work. If you
see one of them gone and the other one's back at about eight-
thirty or nine, you know the wife's usually there. She's just
dropped the kids off to school. (No. 035)

Some subjects also kept an eye on places prior to breaking in
to them to ascertain whether they contained enough valuable
merchandise to make a burglary worthwhile. They inferred

this information from the appearance of the occupants, particularly the clothing and jewelry that they wore (see Merry, 1981).

> If I spot a easy house or something, I got to really check you out first and see what you got. Cause I ain't gon just go in your house and I don't see you dressin' like nothin' or not wearin' no jewelry. You be wastin' my time. (Bill Anderson – No. 050)

Furthermore, a few offenders attempted to collect additional information such as the timing of police patrols, the daily activities of neighbors, and the presence of any extraordinary security precautions. These offenders, however, were the exception; most simply watched places as a way of reducing the chances of anyone being home when they actually committed the burglary.

The practice of watching possible targets prior to attacking them facilitates the commission of residential burglary in situations where offenders find themselves short of cash. When faced with the need to get money quickly, offenders who have a specific target lined up are liable to be especially open to the possibility of committing burglary. After all, once a place has been located and checked out, much of the groundwork has already been completed.

> I wasn't gon to do the house that day, [but] my money got funny. So I had to think of a quick way [of getting some]. So I thought about that one there. (No. 015)

But how do offenders come to be watching these places to begin with? Do they purposely seek them out? Or do they simply stumble on them in the course of their daily rounds? For most of the offenders in our sample who typically watched dwellings before breaking in to them, the answer seemed to fall somewhere between these two extremes. The subjects usually did not go out with the specific intention of looking for potential targets. Nor did they generally just happen upon places when locating prospective burglary sites was the last thing on their minds. Rather they were continually "half looking" for targets. As one put it: "When you out here without a job, you got to keep your eyes and ears open all the time." While not actively seeking targets, these offenders nevertheless remained attuned to their surroundings as they went about their day-to-day, "routine activities" (Felson, 1986:126).

> You could be just coming from somewhere. I might have some business that I got to do in [a nearby municipality] and I'm on the way back home and I see a house. (Jerome Little—No. 064)

> I don't really look for any kind of area, just, I don't know, I don't really go out looking for a house just, like, if I'll see it and it looks good. (Milo Davis—No. 076)

They were aware that they would need to commit additional burglaries in the future but, not needing to do so at the moment, were not motivated to take the necessary steps to locate targets. Viewed in the context of their lives, lives largely oriented toward keeping the party going, this makes perfect sense. From the perspective of the offenders, actively searching for targets that might not be needed for some time was "too much like hard work" and interrupted enjoyment of the moment. Such enjoyment, of course, often entailed loitering with friends on streetcorners and front porches in the neighborhood and this facilitated the process of discovering potential targets.

Nonetheless, some of the subjects who routinely watched their targets prior to offenses actually sought out these places in a more or less systematic fashion. Even in these cases, however, their efforts were usually lackadaisical.

> I might go to the neighborhood park or something and then I might say, "Well, I'm a go home this way today." Then while I'm walkin' up the street I just be lookin', checkin' it out. (No. 057)

I'll say, like, "I'm a walk from [one part of the city to an-other]." And I walk, you know. Then my mind might wan-der, you know. So I might say, "Let me turn here or there," you know, scopin' . . . as I go . . . You know, I might say, "It's nice here" and I write that down . . . Your mind just wanders and you just turn here or turn there and you don't really think about it. (No. 009)

Certainly, none of these subjects searched for potential targets with any marked determination. They went about the task in a casual, unhurried way as befits those who are under no immediate pressure. In this sense, they were not dissimilar from their counterparts who only "half looked" for possible burglary sites. In the end, all of the offenders found dwellings without putting much effort into the process. Indeed, many indicated that promising targets virtually leapt out at them.

I might get up and just ride the bus . . . I ain't saying, "Well, I'm going out here to do a burglary." I might just ride to think where I could do a burglary. Then, as I'm ridin', I say, "Uh oh, there one is!" (No. 018)

But what drew the attention of the offenders to these particu-lar places to begin with? What was it about specific residences that caused the offenders to consider them worth watching?

Almost all of the offenders initially were attracted to resi-dences which, judging from the outside, appeared to them to contain "good stuff" (see Merry, 1981). Conversely, only a few of them were drawn to places simply because they looked easy or safe. This should not be surprising; after all, the offenders made it a practice to watch potential targets for some days before burglarizing them. Thus, they could assess and deal with such matters in the fullness of time. Several externally visible cues suggested to the burglars that a residence con-tained things worth stealing. These cues, of course, were subjective, being judged both in relation to the poor housing conditions in which a majority of the offenders found them-selves living and in light of the realistically available alternatives. The most obvious cue was the size of the structure. Other things being equal, a large house was regarded as promising the biggest payoff.

> If a house is big, it's got some money. A big house, you got to go through all them rooms and you got four or five people stayin' there, so all of them got they own stash; I'm goin' to get it! (No. 009)

Another cue was the condition of the property. Well-maintained dwellings were believed to contain the most desirable goods.

> Well, some [houses] is kept up more than others. Somebody gon put just a little more umph in theirs than anybody else . . . I feel [that one's] got more goodies in there. Not for safety, cause it's probably not safe doin' either one of them. But [the well-maintained one] might have a little bit more. Like, this one might have the same refrigerator, but his got a icemaker on the door. Same refrigerator, but all this guy got to do is put his cup to the door . . . Like I said, if you keep the outside looking nice, then you know the inside is just as good. Cause you got to live on the inside. You want your house to be presented in and outside your house. Now, if you don't give a shit, you let weeds grow. That's people that seldom have company or, if they do, they raunchy people. So you don't want that house. But if you have a up-keeped house and the trash is all put up and the lawn is manicured and the bushes is neatly trimmed and the bird [feeder] got bird seed in it, that's what you want. (No. 018)

The type of car parked in the driveway of a residence also influenced some of the subjects. In their view, an expensive car outside meant valuable property inside.

> Here's this big ol' huge house sittin' up there and in the driveway is two BMWs and a Mercedes. This other house might have a van or something like that . . . So I visualize

that [the intended target] must have more things than that house. (No. 017)

Several of the offenders said they were attracted to residences specifically by BMWs and Mercedes-Benzs rather than by expensive cars generally. In part this probably reflects the fact that these makes are reputed to be popular with successful drug dealers. As noted earlier, many offenders regard places belonging to drug dealers as ideal targets.

On rare occasions, the subjects decided to watch a dwelling because they knew there were valuable goods inside. This information had been obtained fortuitously when they saw new occupants moving in or merchandise being delivered. The offender quoted below did not usually watch targets, but made an exception in this instance because he saw expensive furniture being taken into a house.

[T]hey moved somethin' out and it looked practically brand new; it was a sofa, that's what it was. They had somebody come get a sofa. Then I seen [a well-known regional furniture store] bring another living room set in. Then I said, "This a pretty livin' room set here. These folks got some money." So that's what made me decide to [check them out]. (No. 046)

Residents of high-crime neighborhoods are wary of displaying their household possessions in public for precisely this reason (see Merry, 1981). They often move from one residence to another at night, using the darkness to prevent would-be thieves from getting a glimpse of their personal belongings.

The offenders, then, were drawn to dwellings by what might broadly be termed "reward" cues. But there was more than this at work. A number of the subjects noted that while they were attracted by signs of wealth there was an "extra something" that caused them to select one residence from a group of others that looked quite similar.

All these houses are all like, you know, brightly lit and stuff,
[but] there's like one that's just, you know, not like the others; kinda draws my attention. (No. 076)

I be seeing [the cars outside the house], but it's just something in my mind that say for me to get that house. (No. 017)

It looked like a nice quality house. They all quality houses
in the neighborhood, but this look like a nice one. I can't
tell you 100 percent why I picked it, but it just seemed like
[the one]. (Bernard Smith—No. 066)

Their targets were perceived as special, standing out from the
rest. One offender claimed that some places "asked" to be burglarized: "It's like [they] sayin', 'Come on, get me.' " Katz has
argued that this way of thinking is a conjuring trick by means
of which offenders begin to imbue intended targets with se-
ductive properties as a way of summoning up the motivation
to attack them.

This is not a magic used to trick the audience of observers
who are not in on the magician's sleight of hand; this is a
magic that takes in its magician-creator. In some sense, the
would-be thief is imputing to objects and the scene the sensual capacities to seduce. But, just as obviously, in some
other sense the would-be thief must be accomplishing the
imputation tacitly for the feeling of temptation to be raised.
(Katz, 1988:56)

This argument would seem especially appropriate in the case
of offenders who watch targets prior to burglarizing them. The
time spent watching could facilitate the interactive process of
seduction. Several of the offenders alluded to this process, saying things along the lines of, "The more I looked at it, the
sweeter it looked." House buyers often report a similar experience, in which all the places they looked at met their objective
criteria for an ideal abode, but one rose to the top of their list
because it "felt right."

In short, most of the subjects in our sample usually watched potential targets for some time before committing a burglary. By and large, they were attracted to these targets by external cues suggesting that there were goods worth stealing inside. This finding flies in the face of the results of previous studies indicating that most residential burglars choose targets because they appear to be "safe," that is, well covered and unoccupied (e.g., Bennett and Wright, 1984; Wright and Logie, 1988). Undoubtedly, this difference is due to the fact that these earlier studies contained a large proportion of offenders who searched for targets with the intention of committing an offense there and then. Under such circumstances, offenders *must* be attuned to safety cues; they are not planning to take the time required to assess the risks more fully.

Searching for a Target

Some offenders do not routinely have a potential target available when they decide to do a residential burglary. Ten of the subjects in our sample said that when faced with the pressing need to commit burglary, they usually first had to go out and search for a suitable dwelling to attack.

> Sometime I wake up with a burglary on my mind. I'll wake up thinkin', "Where am I gon get some money from?" . . . I'll wake up early in the mornin'; about five or six in the mornin'; and go out knockin' on doors. I usually find me a house to do. (Howard Ford—No. 014)

> It's nothing like, "Tomorrow we gon sit down here and we gon run in this person's house." We might just be sittin' here like we sittin' now and I'll say, "Let's go to such and such a place." . . . We end up goin' for a ride lookin' for some houses we could get into . . . [And when we find them] we don't just up and say, "Tomorrow we gon get this and that." We just do it [right then]. (William Jones—No. 038)

Virtually all of the offenders said that they occasionally were obliged to locate a vulnerable target and burglarize it immediately. At times, they did not have a potential target lined up or, if they did, it sometimes was unavailable because the occupants were at home. One way around this problem was to search for a dwelling that could be broken in to right then. This solution carried a large element of risk because the offenders knew nothing about the occupants or their daily routine. Accordingly, they approached the selection of such a target with considerable trepidation.

When searching for a residential burglary site, the offenders typically were required to make two basic decisions. First, they had to decide on a suitable area for their search. And second, they had to select a specific target from within this area. What were the factors that underpinned their choices?

In selecting an area, the offenders did not have an infinite supply from which to choose. Both physical and psychological barriers limited their horizons (Brantingham and Brantingham, 1981). Many offenders, for instance, did not have access to a car when the need arose to locate a burglary target. This meant that, for all intents and purposes, they were restricted to areas that were within walking distance. Moreover, this distance could be severely circumscribed, particularly in cases where they hoped to steal heavy or bulky items.

> I ain't gonna go no further than ten blocks; that's a ways to be carryin' stuff . . . Since I'm on foot, I got to keep walkin' back and forth until I get it all. (Howard Davis—No. 020)

> I don't have no car and I don't want to be walking or catching no bus. If I go out in [a distant municipality] and do a burglary, how am I going to get back with all the stuff? (Tom Bryant—No. 026)

> It's hard as hell gettin' on a bus carrying a big picture or a vase. People will look at you like, "Where did he get that from?" or "Where's he going with that?" . . . You subject to get caught. So it's really a [lack of] transportation thing with me. (No. 040)

And even offenders who did have a car sometimes could not travel very far because they were out of money and low on gas.

> [I was out of money and] I didn't have that much gas to really be ridin' far out the way. (No. 014)

The logistical problems posed by committing burglaries a long way from home without reliable transportation became very obvious during our research. On one occasion, an offender was arrested because his car, laden with stolen goods, broke down a short distance from the house he had just burglarized. Unable to start the vehicle and many miles from home, he returned to the target on foot and called for a taxi. When the cab arrived, he filled it with his booty and asked the driver to take him to a spot near his own house. The driver complied but, having become suspicious, called the police immediately after dropping him off. The offender was easily apprehended as he struggled home with the evening's takings.

Beyond the practical constraints, there also were psychological factors that served to restrict the range of areas available to the offenders. As Brantingham and Brantingham (1981:37) have observed, a great deal of the territory that is objectively accessible to criminals is subjectively out-of-bounds, being "unknown . . . [and] populated with the terrors of the unfamiliar." From the offender's perspective, *all* residential burglaries are committed in an environment alive with hazards. But this is especially true where the occupants are not known and the target has not been watched beforehand; there is no reliable way of assessing the risks. Many of the offenders responded to this hazard by conducting their searches for potential burglary sites only in a location with which they already were intimately familiar. They knew the layout of the area and felt comfortable or safe there.

> Basically, all [of my burglaries are committed on the south side of the city]. I guess I know the area. I don't know, I'm comfortable with it I guess . . . I'm basically familiar with it. You know, if it came down to me having to run and stuff

like that, I'd know pretty much where to go. (Bonnie Williams — No. 007)

Perhaps a more important reason, though, was that the offenders had an intuitive understanding of the people who lived in the area. They had a "feel" for what the residents were like. This, they believed, gave them a basis on which to predict the behavior of the local population.

Whenever I decide to do [a burglary], it's always on the north side . . . because I know the people in general . . . , I know they movements. (No. 040)

These offenders had a vested interest in being able to rely on predictions about the habits of the occupants of an intended target. Absent specific information about the occupants, a general familiarity with the sort of people who resided in the area represented the next best means of making such predictions.

In essence, then, the offenders were responding to the hazards inherent in residential burglary by relying on "cognitive maps" to reduce their fear as they searched for targets. Merry (1981:172) has described the way in which residents of high-crime neighborhoods cope with the threat of victimization by developing "cognitive models or maps of places . . . that they view as safe and dangerous. These maps are subjective representations imposed on the physical realities of space . . . , distortions of reality that reflect the individual's past experience and knowledge." She goes on to suggest that cognitive maps encourage people to restrict their activities to areas they know well.

The process of constructing cognitive maps involves drawing distinctions and making generalizations. Maps of areas that are well known are more finely differentiated; maps of unfamiliar areas are broken into larger, less detailed sections. The process parallels the construction of categorical identities. If a person hears about a crime in a familiar area, he may decide that the corner, block, or immediate neighborhood is dangerous, but will not extend this attitude to the entire neighborhood. Hearing of a similar incident in an unfamiliar area, one of the blank spaces on his cognitive map, he is likely to generalize his sense of danger to the entire section since he cannot pinpoint a particular street-corner or street he should avoid. Through this process of generalization, unfamiliar areas gradually acquire a more dangerous reputation, while the same spate of crimes in a familiar area brands only a few corners or blocks as danger-ous. (Merry, 1981:172)

It is ironic that the offenders' cognitive maps constrained their activities in a similar fashion. There was, for example, a marked tendency for black offenders to seek targets only in black areas and for the white offenders to stick mostly to white areas, each group believing that the other's neighbor-hoods were unsafe. They appreciated that, to avoid appearing suspicious, they had to blend in with the local population (see Pettiway, 1982; Reppetto, 1974). As one black subject put it: "You just stay away from [white areas] cause they see you and you look suspicious to them automatically cause, hey, you a new face. 'What you doin' walkin' up and down our street lookin'?' You just try and stay within your confines. Now over here, hey, you see black people walkin' up and down the street all day. No problem." Beyond a desire to be inconspicuous, there was a general perception among the offenders—black and white—that committing offenses in areas populated by a racial group other than their own was too risky. In explaining why such areas were dangerous, they made broad generaliza-tions. One white offender, for instance, said that she avoided looking for targets in black neighborhoods because they were "too wild."

> It's not the fear of the black people that would stop me. Just, I don't know, I guess it would be a little too wild. (No. 007)

Another white subject, though someone who seldom searched for targets, reported staying away from black areas for fear of being shot.

(89)

Oh no! . . . That's one place we don't go . . . [Blacks] see a
white dude walkin' down the street with a VCR, they'll
blow your head off. (No. 085)

And with a similarly sweeping statement, a black offender dismissed the idea of hunting for burglary sites in white neighborhoods because the residents almost invariably kept dogs in
their homes as a crime prevention measure.

I try and stay away from [white areas] because, one thing,
they have a lot of dogs. They keep dogs in the house in case
somethin' happen and, you know, I just try and stay away.
(No. 046)

Interestingly, the white offenders tended to view black neighborhoods as policed more heavily than other places, while the
black subjects typically said that white areas received the
most intensive patrolling.

[White areas have] better police protection as far as they
neighborhoods go, you know, *all* of them got police protection. They cruise and they doin' their job. (No. 046)

Both groups agreed, however, that stealing from dwellings in
white neighborhoods was more lucrative, other things being
equal, than working in black areas. It is not surprising, therefore, that the offenders who reported sometimes crossing racial boundaries in their search for targets were more likely to
be black than white.

You can look for [white people] to have your basics, you
know. Two or three guns, well, maybe one or two guns out
this way. And a couple of rifles. White people hunt a lot
more so than blacks. I don't know nobody that hunts and
I'm thirty-five years old! [They have] jewelry and they keep
it all in one spot. (Bobby Brooks—No. 019)

The subjects, then, perceived areas populated predominantly by another racial group in terms of generalizations
which suggested to them that offending in these areas was too

dangerous. However, they drew much finer distinctions when it came to areas residentially dominated by members of their own race. Within these areas, the subjects had clear ideas about unsafe locations for burglaries; these were micro-level distinctions, sometimes involving just one block of a single street. Many of the burglars wanted to avoid neighborhoods that were heavily patrolled or aggressively policed. As one observed: "You got to stay away from where the police ride real tough." This created an ironic situation in which some offenders were unwilling to hunt for targets in "high crime" areas.

> [I stay away from the neighborhoods like my own because] where I live, I do a burglary and then I get robbed. It's like the police is in my area. Whereas there might be one cop [in another area], there's four in my neighborhood. (No. 019)

In practice, this usually meant staying away from neighborhoods characterized by the open selling of drugs since such areas often are subjected to intense scrutiny by the police. As a member of the sample noted: "You don't want to look in bad neighborhoods where they sellin' dope and all that cause the police ride steady." Police patrols also often are intensified in neighborhoods that have recently experienced a spate of burglaries. Being aware of this, most of the offenders varied the places in which they searched for burglary sites.

> Well, like if I went to [a certain area] today, I wouldn't go tomorrow cause, once the people in [that area] have reported it, [the police] going to be a little bit more on they toes. Not to prevent anything, just to let the people who payin' their salaries to them know that the security is beefed-up. So you have to kind of think like a cop. (No. 019)

One subject, however, preferred to switch to another type of crime rather than to move his activities to a different locale. This offender changed from burglary to armed robbery whenever the police stepped up their patrol in his neighborhood. He reasoned, somewhat counterintuitively, that as his robberies were committed in the open, police patrols were not much of a threat. After all, he could easily see approaching patrol cars and conduct himself accordingly. To his mind, burglaries were more hazardous because, as he put it: "When you're comin' out of that window, you never know who's waitin' on the other side."

As well as avoiding heavily policed areas, most of the offenders wanted to steer clear of neighborhoods in which the residents appeared to be keeping an eye out for each other.

> [Those neighborhoods] are just a hassle. You walk down the street and the police come get you cause somebody done looked out the window and saw you walkin'. (No. 016)

They inferred whether this might be the case from a variety of factors including the general condition of the area and the age composition of its population. Other things being equal, well-kept neighborhoods with a high proportion of elderly residents were viewed by the offenders as poor areas from which to select targets. The residents of such neighborhoods were presumed to be especially vigilant and prone to reporting suspicious-looking persons to the police.

> The thing is, if you got a lot of elderly people on one block, that'll get you killed mostly . . . I wanted to do [a burglary] over here by the bakery shop, but that's a retired area. Almost everybody that live on that block is retired and they constantly lookin' out windows and watchin' [out] for each other. Ain't nothin' you can do about that. (James West — No. 044)

There was considerable disagreement among the offenders about whether a street sign declaring that the residents of an area were participating in a "Neighborhood Watch" scheme indicated that a neighborhood really was being monitored. Certainly, some believed that this was so and avoided offending in these locations.

> Certain areas or certain streets you don't want to mess with cause they have a block watch unit thing. It's a Neighbor-

hood Watch thing, that's what it's called. You don't mess with Neighborhood Watch. You see one of them [signs] in that block, you leave that block alone and you go one or two blocks over. You cruise up and down the street and, if you don't see no Neighborhood Watch thing, then you good to go. [Neighborhood Watch areas are too risky] because if someone's home watchin', say, like in every third home, it's somebody home watchin' the rest of the houses. You know, elderly people, whatever, and all they do is pick up the telephone and make one call — 911 — and there it is. (No. 046)

A lot of times you go in them neighborhoods and they got those [Neighborhood Watch] signs up and they see some people just bumblin' around the neighborhood, they gon call the police on you. (No. 026)

Others, however, took a more cynical view of the signs. One subject, for instance, noted that he lived in a Neighborhood Watch area himself, adding "and there are still a lot of burglaries going on over there. Neighborhood Watch is just something they put up there. You can't watch a neighborhood all day long. They got them signs everywhere. That's not stopping nothing." And another subject claimed that the person who organized the Neighborhood Watch scheme on her street was well-known to local property offenders as someone always willing to buy stolen goods. Offenders such as these were no less concerned than others to avoid being observed by neighbors who were likely to intervene personally or to call the police, but previous experience had convinced them that local Neighborhood Watch areas were not especially risky.

Over our way, them folks ain't gon do nothin' or say nothin'. "Did you see that?" "See what?" Hell, they could be going down the alley with a forty-foot ladder. They just don't want to be involved. So nah, I ain't never had no problem [with Neighborhood Watch]. (No. 020)

In this sense, the decision making of these offenders closely resembled that of the "extremely pragmatic" inner-city robbers described by Murray (1983:117–18): "Their calculations seemed to be based on a hard-headed appreciation of the facts. Real risk of being observed [and] real risk of someone calling the police or intervening . . . loomed largest in their thinking . . . [S]ymbolic evidence of the site's cohesiveness, and symbolic increases in the risk of observation and apprehension seemed to be of little deterrence value." The pervasive view among our group of subjects was epitomized by one who commented: "Yeah, I'm worried about [Neighborhood Watch], long as they really watchin'." His tone left little doubt that he believed that this was seldom the case.

The subjects were largely in agreement about the general characteristics of a safe neighborhood in which to commit residential burglaries. Such a place had to be quiet and infrequently patrolled by the police.

> [A safe place is] a quiet neighborhood . . . where the police don't ride around too often up and down the street. (No. 014)

It also had to appear somewhat affluent.

> I wouldn't say [the area had to be] rich, but a neighborhood with money. (No. 014)

> Where I do my thing at [has] pretty houses, they up-to-date. [The houses] look nice. (No. 020)

Obviously, these characteristics are relative and must be viewed from the perspective of offenders who have only a limited range of areas from which to choose. A neighborhood which they judge to be quiet or affluent might well not be regarded as such by others. This fact, however, does not alter the reality of their decision-making calculus.

Having settled on an area, the offenders next needed to locate a specific target. In doing so, they had to find a place that was acceptable to them in terms of probable reward, potential risk, and ease of access. Moreover, their decision had to be made from the sidewalk or street. Once they had stepped from public to private property, their actions became considerably more vulnerable to challenge. Recognizing this, most were reluctant to approach residences without first making certain that they were viable targets. Practically speaking, therefore, the offenders were committed to carrying out an offense *before* they entered the grounds of an intended burglary site. This fact has largely been overlooked in previous research on residential burglary, but carries important implications for crime prevention measures. For example, offenders typically cannot determine from the street the type of locks fitted to a dwelling. Nor can they see window decals stating that the property inside has been engraved with an identification number. And by the time they are close enough to detect such measures, they often have developed a high degree of commitment to going through with the burglary, come what may. Thus, they may disregard or downplay the significance of these situational factors and elect to carry on with the offense.

In searching for a suitable target, the offenders were initially drawn to residences by many of the same factors that attracted those who typically watched places for a time before burglarizing them. In general, they were most tempted by dwellings that were better maintained or more expensively adorned than others in the area, believing that this was a reliable indicator of potential reward.

> It's the way [the residents] keep the yard, keep it nice and
> trim and have little statues of something out there. You look
> at that and you say, "Hey, this is a well kept up house."
> That tells you that a person spends a little on they property.
> (No. 046)

As these offenders intended to commit an offense immediately upon locating a target, however, factors suggesting that a residence contained valuable goods were insufficient in and of themselves to cause a place to be selected. More importantly, prevailing conditions had to be assessed as being low-risk. The offenders were not willing to break into a dwelling—no matter how lucrative it looked—where they perceived the odds of getting caught to be excessively high.

In assessing risk, the burglars focussed primarily on the issue of occupancy. With few exceptions, they were averse to burglarizing a residence while anyone was inside, and thus were attuned to factors which, in their minds at least, provided some indication of whether the residents were at home. Many situational factors were taken into account by the offenders in making a judgment about occupancy.

> [A car in the driveway might mean someone is in], but if a car is there and you see a lot of leaves piled up [beside it] then the car is not running or these people are not at home. If there's mail in the slot and it's this time of night and you know the mailman ran earlier, either they're not there or they asleep or dead or something. Why else would they not get their mail? (No. 019)

Beyond these factors, however, several offenders mentioned that they simply got "a feeling" about whether or not a place was occupied. The offender quoted above, for instance, added that determining occupancy involved more than rational calculation: "Those are the obvious signs, but there are some other signs that unconsciously come to you. It's basically a feeling you have." Here again, we are encountering a process that the offenders perceived as magical, whereby targets that objectively seemed acceptable took on an added, metaphysical appeal (Katz, 1988).

Burglar alarms and dogs, of course, can function as "occupancy proxies" (Waller, 1979), that is, as substitutes for occupancy by the residents. Therefore, it should come as no surprise that many of the offenders wanted to avoid them.

> If I see an alarm out, like I say, they usually have them outside the house, I'll leave them alone automatically. (No. 046)

> If there's a Rover in [the house], no way we goin' in there. (No. 026)

Alarms, however, seldom are installed on residences containing little of value. Indeed, a few of the offenders regarded the devices not so much as deterrents as indicators of potential reward. Previous experience had convinced them that alarms could be defeated.

> Basically, I look for alarms in certain areas. Like in [an affluent suburb] if they got alarms, then you can look for gold and silver and tea sets. If there's an alarm on the first floor, it probably ain't hooked to the top floor. If it's hooked to the top floor, then it ain't hooked to the attic or it's not hooked to the exhaust system. (No. 019)

In any case, the presence of alarms or dogs often was not easily assessed from the street. This meant that these factors frequently could not enter into the initial target selection process, but rather came into play when the offenders attempted to burglarize the chosen targets.

After occupancy, the subjects generally regarded visibility as the next most important issue in assessing risk. They did not want to be observed while entering or leaving a residence and therefore were drawn to dwellings with access points that could not be seen easily from the street or from surrounding buildings.

> Usually I see how the houses and shit around [the potential target] is. How big the trees are [around the place] and shit like that. (No. 016)

In a related vein, the subjects also were concerned about the possibility of being heard while attempting to break into their intended targets. Accordingly, they would not choose residences that were situated too close to other dwellings.

> If the house is like from here and this is the only space in between . . . then I can't get that one. It's too close together . . . I might have to break a window . . . If you do it quick and hard and fast enough, it won't make much noise. But there's a possibility that you won't hit it right and the whole damn pane will fall out. You just don't want to be caught in those situations. (No. 019)

Concerns about being seen or heard by neighbors ruled out the possibility of finding targets in apartment buildings or public housing projects for a number of subjects. One offender explained his reasons for avoiding such places: "You got all them doors in the hallway. I might be pryin' one open and somebody comes out of another one. Or somebody might hear me."

Even where the risks presented by potential targets were deemed to be acceptable, the offenders still had to ascertain whether they could physically manage to break in. In general, this was regarded as unlikely to present problems. The prevailing sentiment was captured by a subject who pointed out, "As long as houses are made of wood and glass, I can get 'em." Nevertheless, ease of access was taken into account by the offenders as they searched for burglary sites. Door and window locks, since they seldom could be seen from afar, did not feature prominently in initial decisions about how easy it would be to get into prospective targets (see Bennett and Wright, 1984; Wright and Logie, 1988). If locks were considered at all, this usually occurred at a later stage. On the other hand, two other things affecting ease of access—security bars and storm windows—often could be seen from a distance. Most of the offenders preferred to avoid both.

> [I stay away from houses] that have windows, doors, and basements and everything barred down. I don't even try to deal with them bars cause I ain't got that much patience. (No. 020)

> I wouldn't mess with a house that has storm windows. I'm not gon say I've never done a house with storm windows, but it just takes more time tryin' to do two windows. (No. 014)

The burglars seemed more unwilling than unable to overcome such obstacles; they just did not want to take the extra time and effort required. Since they were under pressure to act as quickly as possible, this makes sense. Add to this the fact that those who search for burglary sites with the intention of offending "there and then" have no foolproof way to predict the likely payoff, and the aversion to well-protected places is more sensible still. Why should they invest extraordinary energy where the reward cannot be guaranteed?

In summary, while few of the offenders in our sample routinely had to search for a target in order to commit a residential burglary, nearly all of them occasionally had to do so. On these occasions, the search was facilitated by their personal knowledge and beliefs about good and bad areas, as well as by their skill, built up through experience, in reading the cues relating to risks, possible rewards, and ease of access. This combination of knowledge and skill perhaps was what caused the offenders to view the commission of a residential burglary as a feasible means of dealing with a pressing problem in the absence of a preexisting target. They possessed the "know-how" to locate a burglary site on short notice and this allowed them to consider the prospect of breaking in to a dwelling (see Lofland, 1969:82–84).

Seizing an Opportunity

In the popular imagination, residential burglars are usually thought of as "opportunistic" offenders. Certainly, this is how they are portrayed in the crime prevention literature produced by police and other organizations. There is no consensus, however, regarding what qualifies a criminal as an opportunist (Bennett and Wright, 1984), though common sense would suggest that such an offender is one who "just happens upon" a vulnerable target and, as a result, commits an offense on the spur of the moment. And by this definition, only one of the offenders in our sample might reasonably be considered opportunistic. Typically his burglaries were committed immediately following the chance discovery of an unprotected dwelling.

Yeah, [I'm an opportunist] cause I find myself walkin' down the street with no intentions on doing a burglary. But I may

(99)

see somebody leavin' the house and, at that time, the idea
[to break in] may pop in my head, right at that instant. I may
look at the house first and see what kind of house it is . . .
See just how I can get in there. Lot of times I may do it right
there on the spot. (No. 013)

This is not to suggest that the remaining offenders had never
done a residential burglary under similar circumstances; as
noted in chapter 2, a number of them told us about offenses
that could only be described as opportunistic. One burglar, for
example, was waiting for a bus when he saw a man and
woman, carrying suitcases, come out of a nearby house, get in
a car and drive off. Reasoning that these were the occupants
and that they were going out of town, he broke into the dwelling. He said that he had not been thinking about burglary, but
that this was "too good an opportunity to pass up." When and
where such opportunities would occur, however, was unpre-
dictable, and the offenders could not count on one presenting
itself in times of immediate need. Not surprisingly, therefore,
they usually relied on a more proactive strategy to locate potential burglary sites.

Overall, then, it is misleading to label the subjects we interviewed as opportunists, even though many of them occasionally had exploited opportunities that cropped up in the course
of their daily rounds (see Cromwell et al., 1991). Interestingly,
all of the opportunistic burglaries described by those in our
sample were precipitated by the fortuitous sighting of people
leaving a residence. Putting it another way, not one offense
was prompted by the discovery of an open door or window.
More than anything, this probably reflects the fact that, first
and foremost, the majority of offenders are concerned with occupancy; they do not want to attack a dwelling while the residents are inside. Therefore, the sight of people leaving a place
can represent a powerful temptation. Conversely, although an
open door or window may suggest ease of access, it also may
indicate that someone is at home. And few offenders are prepared to gamble in these circumstances.

Summary

When faced with a pressing problem, financial or otherwise, that needed to be resolved quickly, a majority of the offenders typically had a potential residential burglary target already lined up. This involved not merely having a specific dwelling in mind, but also possessing reliable information about such things as the routine of its occupants. In most cases, the target initially had been located during the course of the offender's daily activities and then casually kept under surveillance for a period of time. Sometimes, though, the target was selected because the offender either knew the occupants personally or else had received a tip from someone with inside knowledge of the place. In these cases, there was no need to watch the residence before burglarizing it; the offender already had satisfactory intelligence. Regardless of the way in which the potential target was located, however, its very availability served to facilitate the commission of a residential burglary by making the offense that much more "proximate and performable" (Lofland, 1969:61).

Only a few of the offenders usually found themselves without a possible residential burglary site when under pressure to act in response to an immediate need. Many of them, however, occasionally were in this position. Even here, though, the offenders almost invariably had a clear idea of how to locate a promising target without undue risk or difficulty. This facilitated the commission of a residential burglary in much the same way as did having a specific target lined up.

That the offenders, at the time of actually contemplating a residential burglary, typically had a target fully assessed and "waiting in the wings," has at least two important implications for attempts to prevent their crimes. First, it suggests that they often had direct knowledge regarding matters such as household security and the daily routine of occupants and, therefore, were somewhat immune to symbolic measures designed to confuse them (e.g., by creating the illusion of occupancy). Second, it indicates that they generally possessed a more realistic basis on which to judge risk than is commonly imagined, evidence that might weaken the case for the inhibiting influence of threatened sanctions. These are matters that will receive further attention in the next chapter.

4 Entering the Target

ONCE OFFENDERS HAVE SELECTED a specific residential burglary target, they confront the task of actually breaking into the place. At first glance, this may appear to be a fairly simple matter. On closer investigation, however, it proves to be quite challenging, involving a set of actions that have to be performed in the face of a "problematic outcome and potentially serious consequences" (Shover, 1991:103). Not only must offenders deal with physical obstacles designed to frustrate their efforts, they must do so under considerable emotional pressure in an environment alive with potential hazards. How, then, do they accomplish this feat? That is the question to which this chapter will be devoted. This matter has attracted little criminological research, but it has important implications for our understanding of offender decision making. Such decision making does not end with the selection of a target; indeed, the decision to commit a residential burglary is itself subject to reversal, at least in theory, until the offender has actually completed the process of getting into that target.

Having settled on a residence, there is a natural tendency for offenders to feel compelled to get the burglary over and done with. In part, this is probably a product of their initial motivation; after all, they typically are contemplating the offense in response to a pressing need and therefore are predisposed to quick action. But there is another aspect of the situation that contributes to this heightened sense of urgency. The offenders are on the brink of a risky venture and, recognizing this, are inclined to become increasingly tense and agitated (Bennett and Wright, 1984). One way in which they can effectively deal with this anxiety is simply to move ahead, thereby putting the source of their unease behind them. Indeed, the offenders in our sample often adopted just such a strategy.

> I don't know if you ever stole anything in your life; it's a mixture of fear and anxiety and just excitement; it's adrenaline pumping through your body . . . Even if we haven't cased out these houses as much as we would've liked to [we just do them]. But it's because we're up and our adrenaline is pumping and we want to just get it and get it done. (No. 100)

> Ain't no hesitation involved in [burglary]; he who hesitates sometimes is lost. That hesitation could be the police comin' by or a neighbor comin' by and, if you had gone when you first wanted to, it could be over with by now. (Larry Williams — No. 037)

Paradoxically, though, some offenders were inhibited from moving ahead by the very anxiety that impelled them to action. Finding themselves in a state of near paralysis, they often used drugs with the express purpose of summoning up the courage to proceed (see Cromwell et al., 1991). The drug of choice, however, varied from offender to offender.

[A shot of heroin] pumps you up. You talk about pumpin'
up, that pumps you up: "Go get it! Ain't nobody gon see
you. Fuck 'em." (No. 012)

I smoke [crack cocaine], man . . . [I]f I went [to do a burglary]
straight, I wouldn't have the balls to do it. (No. 031)

[Smoking marijuana] might give me a reaction like pushing
me into doing what I want to do. (No. 032)

As the crime got underway, with events accelerating and
taking on a life of their own, outside concerns became increasingly attenuated; the offenders turned far more serious, focussing intently on surreptitiously getting into the target.

You just thinking [about] one thing, this thing that you're
doing. (Rob Newhouse – No. 070)

Goin' in, all you be thinking about is gettin' in. (No. 064)

This usually required them to move progressively through
three stages, each of which had to be completed without attracting suspicion: (1) approaching the building; (2) making a
final check for occupancy; and (3) effecting an entry.

Approaching the Target

Offenders are aware that in stepping from public to private
property, they become much more vulnerable. Whereas people
walking or driving down a public street are unlikely to draw
attention to themselves – especially within areas residentially
dominated by members of their own race – the burglars' actions suddenly are open to challenge when they enter residence grounds. Many offenders became quite nervous at this
point and literally could not continue until they got their emotions under control.

That's when I be making my split decisions; should I or
should I not? I'm thinking about it for maybe about five

minutes. I look at the house again and might walk past it
and walk back, then go for it. (Bob Hill—No. 021)

Yeah, [I'm] just a little nervous . . . Then I just hit my mind
and clear it out. You know, I take a real deep breath. Now
I'm relaxed and before my nerves come back up . . . hey, I'm
goin'. (No. 009)

Beyond this, the subjects had another reason for wanting to
keep their emotions reined in. Katz (1988:59) has observed
that all offenders embarking on what he calls sneaky property
crimes quickly realize that they "must work to maintain a
conventional, calm appearance" to be successful. This observation applies to those we interviewed, several of whom commented on the need to behave in a casual, confident, or natural
way when approaching potential targets.

When I do a burglary, I know what I'm going to do. I know
who I'll hit. I know what time to hit. So I'm going to look
real casual. I'm not going up there . . . looking around and
seeing who's watching me. (No. 079)

You're a little nervous every time you do it . . . [A]fter a
while, you just walk in with confidence. But you're always
nervous; you never get rid of that. (No. 083)

You don't want to go in a place thinking things that will
upset you. You got to be natural, man; walk up to the house
like it's yours. You got to look natural. [If the] police ride by
man, wave at 'em . . . You don't want to do nothing that
draws suspicion; being nervous is how you get caught. (No.
064)

Behaving "naturally" was quite problematic for the subjects
in light of the fact that they were cognizant of their real motives and concerned about giving themselves away (Matza,
1969). As Katz has noted, offenders often find it difficult to
perform mundane activities in situations where they must do
so in order to disguise their deviant intentions.

Sensing a difference between what appears to be going on
and what is "really" going on, the [offender] focuses intently
on normal interactional tasks. Everyday matters that have
always been easily handled now rise to the level of explicit
consciousness and seem subtle and complex. (Katz, 1988:59)

A number of the offenders typically adopted a ruse to make
it easier for them to project a "normal" appearance as they
approached intended targets. Some, for example, donned work
clothes and pretended to be service technicians, house build-
ers or painters.

> [I dress up as] some type of service man or electrician or
> somethin' like that. I never go as a plainclothes man doin'
> anything. (No. 017)

> [I go] just like I'm dressed now, [wearing overalls covered
> with paint]. I could go and break in your house and won't
> nobody know nothin'; they think I'm workin' on your
> house. (No. 012)

A few acquired a van—sometimes legally, sometimes not—
and disguised themselves as delivery persons or house movers.

> [We use a van from a well-known furniture rental company].
> The van [with a company name on it] pulls up, one person
> stays in the van supposedly doing paperwork and the other
> person goes around back . . . Let's say a neighbor does look
> out and see; what do they see? They see a [furniture rental
> company] van pull up. (No. 100)

One subject took her young children along on some burglaries,
leaving them in the car as she went up to the residence. She
reasoned that the presence of the youngsters made her appear
to onlookers as a "respectable" person whose motives were
above suspicion. As she put it: "[If] the neighbors or somebody
sees me, I got a lot of children around—taking them to school
or picking them up—and this is what the neighbors see; so
they aren't aware of what [I'm doing]."

Other offenders avoided the need to maintain a conventional appearance by approaching their targets under the cover of darkness (see Lofland, 1969) or bad weather.

> I won't do a burglary in the daytime. At one time I used to do it, when I was younger. But now, broad daylight, I won't do it. (No. 013)

> On rainy days or days like that, you don't have to worry about police ridin' up or down the street or neighbors bein' nosy. (No. 037)

This is not to suggest, however, that these offenders would be unmindful of their appearance. Almost all of them took great care to wear dark clothing when committing their offenses so that they would blend in with the surroundings and be difficult to spot.

Despite such precautions, it was not unusual for the burglars to be confronted by a neighbor as they were about to attack a residence. On these occasions, they were forced to "think fast" and concoct a plausible story which explained their presence on the property and obscured their true purpose. They sought to remain calm and matter-of-fact, lest they arouse greater suspicion.

> [I]f one of the neighbors happen to come by, then you just give them a fake name and say, "Oh, I was lookin' for so and so. Does he still live here?" "Nah, missus so and so been livin' there for years. They don't have no children, they grandchildren and everything is gone." I say, "Oh, okay, thank you. I got the wrong house then." You know; then you just leave. (No. 046)

> [W]e was still staying in this apartment complex and a neighbor saw me and he opened up the door. He said, "What you doin' over here in this hallway?" I immediately said I was waitin' for so and so. (No. 044)

Katz (1988:58) has suggested that events like these typically interfere with the ability of offenders to construct "a sense that [they] might get away with it." In this regard, such unexpected confrontations might be compared to the breaking of a trance. Suddenly the subjects no longer were engrossed in the mechanics of carrying out the offense and were free to consider alternative courses of action. Certainly, they had to abandon their plan to attack that particular dwelling, at least for the time being.

> [I]t doesn't [always] go as you planned because you run into complications on the property . . . When it comes to a situation where it seems like the risks are going up, then it's time to leave. (John Roberts – No. 041)

Some typically treated any sort of unanticipated confrontation as a bad omen and temporarily gave up on the idea of breaking into a dwelling, without seriously considering the possibility of immediately carrying out a burglary against another target.

> I just said it wasn't meant for me to do [a burglary] today; try and be greedy, that's when you get caught. (No. 049)

> I go home and count my blessings . . . You got to get over that spooked feeling [before doing someplace else]. If I had . . . went on I would've been caught because I didn't pay attention to my first mind. (No. 036)

> [I] gave [residential burglary] up for about two weeks, said, "Fuck it, it must not have been my time." (No. 066)

Others were reluctant to offend elsewhere because they usually did not have another burglary site lined up and felt that it was too risky to commit an offense without first collecting some information about the intended target. For these offenders, locating an alternative target and burglarizing it there and then was not a viable option.

> Nah, I just went home. You can't just say, "Well, I'll take this house today [instead]." You got to have something in mind on why you able to hit this house and what's in there. (No. 027)

We got [the house] eventually, but we couldn't do it that night. I didn't do another one [instead] because I didn't have nothing up; I didn't know what was in the house or what. (No. 067)

In spite of such concerns, many of the offenders occasionally found themselves under so much financial pressure that they had little choice but to locate another burglary target and attack it immediately. As one explained: "Of course, I [found another place to break into], I needed to commit that burglary so bad that day." When this happened, the difficulties inherent in remaining calm while approaching potential burglary sites were compounded by the fact that the offenders often knew little or nothing about the place selected and thus were walking into unknown territory.

In short, the offenders typically experienced considerable anxiety as they approached intended burglary targets. This anxiety had to be firmly suppressed, lest outward signs of nervousness betray their illicit intentions to those who might intervene or call the police. The ability to project a calm appearance under pressure is a requisite skill for the successful commission of residential burglaries. Those who seek to commit such crimes not only have to possess technical "know-how," they also must be able to handle their own emotions (see Walsh, 1986).

Checking for Occupancy

That most offenders are reluctant to burglarize occupied dwellings is beyond dispute. Previous research consistently has demonstrated this (Bennett and Wright, 1984; Cromwell et al., 1991; Rengert and Wasilchick, 1985; Shover, 1991; Walsh, 1980a), and our study reinforces this conclusion. Almost nine out of ten of the offenders that we asked about this issue said that they *always* avoided breaking into a residence when they knew or suspected that someone was at home.

If I even got that feeling that somebody's in the house, I'm
not going in there. (Glenda Harris — No. 042)

I don't never break in nobody's house while [somebody is]
in there. I don't want nobody in there. (No. 047)

I mean you gotta make sure [the residents are] not home;
make sure they're not home. (Tina Smith — No. 092)

What is more, most of the remaining offenders *typically*
stayed away from occupied premises, burglarizing such places
only where extraordinary circumstances made it appear safe
for them to do so. One, for example, explained: "I have [done
places while the occupants were there], but they had been partying and were passed out." Another offender recounted a burglary committed against a casual acquaintance after helping
him stagger home from a lounge in an alcohol-induced stupor.
In cases like these, the dwellings might be thought of as "effectively unoccupied" since the residents were in no condition
to present a threat to intruders.

Cromwell (quoted in Dingle, 1991:98) has implied that burglars, being generally "shy," do not want to attack occupied
homes in part because they are unwilling to risk hurting anyone. Most of the offenders in our sample, however, showed
little concern for the well-being of their victims. In fact, several of them said that they were prepared to use violence
against anyone who got in their way during the commission
of an offense.

When [the occupants] come in there, they better have some
boxing gloves on cause I'm gon whip some ass or somethin'
and I ain't lyin'. It's gon be a fight up in there, partner. You
ain't callin' nobody. You be callin' somebody, it be 911 for
ambulance for your ass cause I'm gon do you. I'm gon hurt
you, I ain't lyin'. Don't come in there and y'all catch me.
Hey man, I'm for real. (No. 011)

Admittedly, we encountered a few persons who said that they
avoided burglarizing occupied places for fear of injuring some-

one. Even these offenders, though, seemed to be driven less by worries about the welfare of the residents than by a desire to escape the possibility of being charged with a more serious offense.

> [If an occupant gets hurt], then you do have a problem; then you got big trouble. So, nah, you leave [occupied residences] alone. It's not worth it to hurt anybody. (No. 035)

> [The residents] can scream, holler, yell, bust your ass or shoot you or you got to shoot them or beat them up. Then, if they die, you goin' to jail for murder. If they don't die, you goin' for attempted assault. (Jade—No. 023)

It strains credulity to argue that the offenders stayed away from occupied dwellings mainly out of compassion or concern for the safety of the residents. Rather, they typically sought to avoid breaking into such places where the risks were perceived as excessively high.

One of the most serious risks faced by residential burglars is the possibility of being injured or killed by the occupants of a target. Many of the offenders we spoke to reported that this was far and away their greatest fear (see Wright and Rossi, 1986).

> I don't think about gettin' caught, I think about gettin' gunned down, shot or somethin' . . . Cause you get into some people's houses . . . quick as I come in there, boom, they hit you right there. That's what I think about. (No. 009)

> Hey, wouldn't you blow somebody away if someone broke into your house and you don't know them? You hear this noise and they come breakin' in the window tryin' to get into your house, they gon want to kill you anyway. See, with the police, they gon say, "Come out with you hands up and don't do nothing foolish!" Okay, you still alive, but you goin' to jail. But you alive. You sneak in somebody's house and they wait til you get in the house and then they shoot

you . . . See what I'm sayin'? You can't explain nothin' to nobody'; you layin' down in there dead! (No. 018)

A person could be up in there, anything. What would I do if somebody is up in there, just standing behind the door with a butcher knife or anything, you know? . . . Like I said, sometimes I don't think about the police . . . I rather for the police to catch me versus a person catching me breaking in their house because the person will kill you . . . Sometimes the police will tell you, "You lucky we came before they did." (No. 069)

Some also said that they often avoided occupied targets because the offenders were known to the residents. As one put it: "Nine times out of ten, I know the people, so I can't let them see me." Moreover, a few offenders refused to attack places while anyone was inside believing that to do so, in and of itself, would make them vulnerable to a more serious criminal charge.

It do matter [if the occupants are home]. I mean that's not burglary, that's robbery if they there. It changes to what? First degree burglary, strong arm, some kinda case they change it to. You don't want nobody to be there, man. (No. 067)

It is testimony to the depth of feeling among the offenders that targets should be unoccupied that, even where they were virtually certain that the residents were away, the vast majority of them nevertheless carried out a last minute check to make certain that no one was inside. This could be done in one of several ways, the most common of which involved knocking on the door or ringing the doorbell (see Walsh, 1980a).

[The target] wasn't too far from where I stay. I knew [the occupant] was gone; matter of fact, he was kind of like a friend of mine . . . We went down the street and I knocked on the door like I was lookin' for him. Ain't nobody come to the door, so [we went ahead with the offense]. (Kelvin Perry—No. 043)

This approach provided the offenders with a fairly reliable means of checking not only for human occupancy, but for the presence of dogs as well.

[N]ine times out of ten you can tell if a dog is in the house or not because [when you walk up to the door], they'll start barking. (No. 071)

The offenders appreciated, however, that people were not always in a position to come to the door immediately. Many of them attempted to compensate for this by knocking or ringing the doorbell continuously or repeatedly for a considerable period of time.

Well, we like, uh, got outta the car and . . . we rang the doorbell like a whole bunch of times. Like, that way, if they were there, they would come down and answer it. (No. 076)

[W]e rung the doorbell and stood there for a few minutes; didn't nobody come. So we always keepin' ahead so we sayin', "They might be in the bathtub or the shower or anything . . . Might just don't want to be bothered." So we go around to the back and knock on the door and stand there a few minutes too. (No. 018)

This tactic increased the risk because the longer the offenders stood on the doorstep, the more chance they had of arousing suspicion. One offender explained: "I knock on the door, [but] you can't be around the house for a long time because people start wondering what you doing and start watching you." No matter how persistent the offenders were, there remained the possibility that the occupants purposely were not coming to the door because they were too lazy, too busy, or too frightened to do so. It also was possible that the residents were pretending not to be home and were lying in wait for intruders. While the odds of this actually happening would seem to be remote, several of the offenders regarded it as a danger.

It might be somebody in there hiding and let you come on in; some people do that, they sit back and watch you. If they see you coming in, they know what you up to — burglary. So they'll go and hide or they won't answer the door or whatever. And then they get you! (No. 026)

[People whose houses have been burglarized before] know the rules of the knockin' on the door thing and they be quiet. (No. 009)

You might get in [a dwelling] and somebody layin' for you, cause I'll do that myself . . . You dyin', cause you goin' in these people's house and it might be somebody that might crack a window for you to come in there and be layin' in there with a shotgun and blow your head off. (No. 045)

Whenever the occupants did answer the door, the offenders had to come up with a convincing reason for being on the doorstep. Most of them pretended to be looking for a friend's house, claiming to be confused as to the exact address (see Walsh, 1980a).

[If] someone comes to the door I say, "Is Ralph here?" "Ralph who?" "Ralph Bakerson." Then I start describing him . . . Then they say, "Oh, I think I know who you talking about. He lives a couple of doors down on the next block. I seen the guy, but I don't know him by name." You see, I done made them see this guy in they head. So I say, "Okay, thank you." Then, as I'm leaving, I'm saying, "I thought this was the address he gave me." (No. 018)

Having now been seen by a resident, many of the offenders felt compelled to abandon the idea of burglarizing that or any other nearby dwelling, realizing that they could be linked to the offense.

To avoid such problems, a number of the subjects elected to telephone residences before attacking them. They thereby could ascertain whether places were occupied without "putting themselves on view." The most common tactic was to

call targets from a nearby public telephone and, if no one answered, to leave the receiver off the hook with the phone still
ringing. This allowed the subjects to approach dwellings with
confidence; the sound of a ringing phone provided an almost
foolproof signal that no one was inside. To employ this strategy, the subjects obviously had to know the telephone number
of their intended target. Some of them typically were acquainted with the occupants and already knew the number.

> So far [I always have burglarized places where I know the
> people] because you know what time they leave and what
> time they get back and sometimes you know they number.
> We might call them or somethin' and see if they there. (No.
> 050)

Others obtained the number by getting the surname of the residents from the mailbox and then looking it up in the local
telephone book or by using a well-known directory that lists
phone numbers by address.

Several offenders checked for occupancy by employing a
slight variation on this tactic; rather than telephoning the intended target, they called the residents at work. They viewed
this as preferable because it not only presumptively indicated
whether the residence was presently unoccupied, it also let
them know the precise location of the occupants and gave
them a rough idea of how long they could spend in the
dwelling.

> I knew this girl and her husband and I knew they both
> worked. I [also] knew where they worked at. I called out to
> their job and found out they was at work . . . [I went to their
> house and broke in. I didn't knock first] cause I knew they
> was at work; wasn't nobody there, they don't have nobody
> there. See, they live by themselves and they don't trust no-
> body being in their house with that [cocaine] in their house.
> I just didn't care. I knew they was at work cause I had just
> called and it wasn't even thirty minutes [earlier]. It don't

even take me fifteen minutes to get to their house from my house. (No. 069)

A few offenders were not deterred by the fact that a dwelling was currently occupied. Most of them broke into places while the occupants were asleep. They reasoned that there was an advantage in doing so; after all, they knew the residents were in, knew exactly where they were and what they were doing, and thus were unlikely to be surprised by them. Two of the offenders commented that breaking into dwellings while the occupants were inside made the offense more exciting. As one said: "[It] adds a little adventure." The other offender claimed that although he usually chose unoccupied targets, he enjoyed burglarizing places where the residents not only were in, but were wide awake. He described such crimes as "a thrill."

> If you can get in while they woke, I prefer they be awake as opposed to them being sleep because you can see them; that's a thrill! To be in a house—a total stranger—you don't know where the gun at, they do, and you stealing. See what I'm sayin', you stealing. (No. 019)

Lofland (1969:114) has suggested that for some offenders crime itself can become job-like and, in their eyes, boring. One way in which they attempt to prevent this from happening, he asserts, involves taking more chances: "[A]cts of theft apparently can get to be very safe affairs, so that if a sense of adventure is to be produced, they must be pursued under conditions of intentionally contrived detection risks." This may explain why a few offenders purposely sought out occupied premises to attack. Such an explanation is consistent with the observation that most of those we spoke to were committed to a lifestyle characterized by the quest for excitement and an openness to "illicit action."

In summary, most of the offenders in our sample wanted to make absolutely certain that dwellings were unoccupied before they attacked them. They obtained this information by

employing the same techniques that law-abiding citizens use
when they want to find out if someone is home; they knocked
on the door, rang the bell, or used the telephone. The offenders
did not require special knowledge or skills to determine occupancy. As Lofland (1969:83) has observed, "much conventional socialization is at the same time an inverse education
for [criminality]."

Effecting an Entry

Once offenders have satisfied themselves that occupancy
does not present a problem, there is little reason for further
delay. After all, they typically are under pressure to act, have
selected a target, and believe that conditions for the crime are
favorable; there is nothing to be gained, and potentially much
to be lost, by waiting.

> Once you got [the place] cased and got the information, what
> you got to think about now? You think too long, then some-
> body's gonna come back and you ain't gon be able to do
> nothing. (No. 022)

It is time for them to "get busy," that is, to effect an entry.
For most offenders, this is the moment of greatest anxiety. It
represents the last point at which they could turn back without having committed a criminal offense. And it also represents the first point at which they could encounter serious
risks, including the possibility of being caught, injured, or
killed. Nevertheless, they must continue to maintain their
composure: their actions remain open to public view, at least
potentially, and they do not want to arouse suspicion. The
challenge is for them to project a conventional appearance
while going about the task of getting into the prospective target (Katz, 1988).

Virtually all of the offenders in our sample agreed that in
order to convey a conventional appearance it was crucial to
avoid any hint of hesitation. From their perspective, appearing
hesitant risked inviting unwelcome attention from neighbors,

passers-by or, worse yet, the police. Accordingly, most of them did not want to stand outside a target looking for the best way to get into that particular place. Rather they preferred to operate on the basis of rules of thumb derived from past experience.

> [M]ostly doors are locked, so there's that right there — you ain't gonna get in. Okay, so never . . . go for the door cause door is usually gonna be locked, just go right for the window. And don't hesitate! Don't hesitate, you know, like standing around the back of the house, "Should we do it? Shouldn't we do it?" If you're there, do it! Okay? (Jhon Do — No. 087)

Through trial and error the offenders had developed "cognitive scripts" (Forgas, 1979; Rumgay, 1992), essentially routinized mental blueprints that established the way in which targets should be entered. The scripts allowed them to move forward confidently and without undue delay despite the fact that they were under considerable stress. However, the scripts employed by the offenders varied widely. Some called for an entrance through the front door, while others prescribed the use of a rear window. But all had one thing in common; they were oriented toward keeping the offenders from being noticed, though they did not invariably involve actions designed to prevent the offenders from being *seen*. In fact, a number of the offenders relied on scripts that directed them to enter dwellings in full public view, using routine or normalcy as a cover so as not to arouse the curiosity of possible onlookers. Subjects who possessed a key to prospective targets, for instance, often approached these places openly, rang the bell and, if no one answered, entered by inconspicuously unlocking the door. They reasoned that anyone happening to see them most likely would pay little attention, concluding perhaps that they lived there, that they were house guests, or that the occupants had let them in. Similarly, several of the offenders used special tools that allowed them to break front door locks, while appearing to be using a key to unlock the door.

[W]e would go and knock on the door, ring the doorbell, nobody would answer, [so we would] take a pair of channel
locks, if it wasn't a dead bolt lock, . . . and just turn [the door
handle] and walk on in like we was going in with a key.
(No. 083)

Locks play a hell of a part [in discouraging burglars], but . . .
[if] you got the right tools, you could go up to the door and
open it up as quickly and as easy as if you had your own key.
So whoever would be looking wouldn't notice anything.
(No. 019)

Many of the offenders believed that they were unlikely to attract much notice where they were seen simply to open the
front door and walk in. After knocking or ringing, therefore,
they often tried the door in the hope that it was unlocked.
Sometimes they were lucky. However, this was more the exception than the rule and, typically, they had to resort to an
alternative method of entry.

I tried the front door and it was locked, so I went around the
back . . . and the back door was locked . . . so I used a coat
hanger and got the door open. (John Doe – No. 077)

Notwithstanding the fact that some offenders habitually
broke into dwellings in such a way that their actions were
visible, most wanted to reduce the chances of being seen to an
absolute minimum. Accordingly, one of their major concerns
was to locate an access point that could not easily be seen
from the street or from neighboring buildings. This was true
for many—though not all—of the offenders who typically
committed their crimes under the cover of darkness or bad
weather. The best-concealed entrance usually was to be found
at the back of a residence, with the target itself shielding the
burglar from view.

[At the back] you got a better shot, you know. So the people
won't call the police, you go to the back door. You know, go

to the front door and everybody see you. Then they identify
you. (No. 006)

Obviously, street people on the street and cars and everything come through and see the front of the house. Who's
gon to see the back of people's houses to see what's goin'
on? Ain't too many people goin' to the back of the house.
(No. 018)

It's too obvious on the front. See, on the back it's not that
obvious. The other . . . houses ain't facing the back. You
don't find too many [potential onlookers] on the back, you
mostly find them on the front. (James Wallace—No. 033)

The offenders, however, were prepared to be flexible when the
situation demanded it, and sometimes broke in at other locations, provided that conditions permitted them to do so without being seen.

I would have gone in from the back ideally, but I noticed
that someone could see me from the back. So I looked at the
front and I definitely would have got busted [there]. So I figured I'd go, like, in [at the side]. (No. 032)

I never [break in] through the front, unless I go through, like,
a porch or something that could hide me. (No. 054)

A popular alternative to entering at the back involved getting
into the garage—which often was left open or unlocked—and
gaining access to the residence through a connecting door.

Nine times out of ten, the houses we break in got garages
and they have, like, doors on the inside of the garage leading
to the house. That's how we used to get in. (No. 071)

Once inside a garage, the offenders were well-covered and
could set about breaking into the place in privacy. As one of
them told us: "Once you get [into] the garage, you can basically do anything you want to do."
  Having settled on an access point that provided sufficient
protection from public view, the offenders next confronted the

problem of overcoming whatever security hardware was present. For the most part, this required them to contend with nothing more complicated than various sorts of household locks (see Shover, 1991). Depending on the type of lock, however, this obstacle could be more troublesome than it might appear on the surface. "Dead bolt" locks, in particular, were almost universally disliked, being strong and difficult to disable.

> I don't do dead bolt locks because sometimes you have to kind of kick the door, loosen it up. I don't really like playing with dead bolts cause it takes too long. On picking locks, you can't really pick a dead bolt lock. (No. 103)

> If you look at [the door] and you see dead bolt locks, then you try not to bother it cause it's more trouble than it's going to be worth. (No. 019)

Nevertheless, some offenders said that they had confidence in their ability to defeat dead bolt locks. One, for example, claimed to have what he referred to as a "dead pull," a device which enabled him to undo such locks. Others reported using some sort of "jimmy," usually a crowbar or large screwdriver, to pry doors from their frames, thereby rendering the locks useless.

> [Dead bolt locks are] discouraging, but you can almost bet that if they got dead bolt locks, then they still got the wood [door frames]; it's just securing the door . . . more than keeping me out. You know what a burglary tool looks like? It looks like a small crowbar and it's thinner. That whole paneling or the siding that keeps the dead bolt into it, that's comin' off, man, that's nothing! (No. 019)

Still others mentioned overcoming dead bolt locks by breaking them with a sledgehammer—an effective, if noisy, tactic.

A majority of the offenders, however, preferred to avoid dead bolt locks and, upon encountering them, usually decided to break in through a window.

If I was to go to a house that got . . . double locking dead bolt locks, nine times out of ten I'm a go in through a window. (No. 013)

If it's a dead bolt lock on . . . every door, then I'll see about going through a window. (No. 058)

Occasionally, the burglars were lucky enough to discover an unlocked window that was accessible and well screened from public view. More typically, they were unable to find an insecure window and had to choose between two alternative methods of entry. The first involved forcing or prying the window open.

[With some kinds of windows] you can take a screwdriver and you can, uhm, right where the window's set into the frame, you can bend the frame back and the window come unclosed. (No. 002)

This method, however, could not be used on all types of windows and, even when it could be used, it had the disadvantage of being time-consuming. Accordingly, many of the offenders turned to the second method; breaking the window. This presented difficulties of its own in that the sound of breaking glass might arouse the curiosity of neighbors or passers-by. Appreciating this, many offenders took steps to muffle the sound. A popular way involved masking the window with tape prior to breaking it.

I got me some tape and taped that window right there, so when you break it you won't hear nothin' and won't nothin' fall. You pull that [tape] off with the glass . . . and go on in there. Just like that! See, you put the tape there and break that window and ain't nothin' gon happen; you won't hear nothin' breakin'. (No. 046)

What we [did] was . . . we took some tape [and] put it over the window real tight. Then we busted it and then we took the tape down and the window was shattered. It had no window in it! (No. 092)

Chapter 4

Another common method was to cover the window with a newspaper, a coat or a blanket before breaking it. Although this technique allowed broken glass to fall to the ground, it was fairly effective in muffling the sound created by shattering the window.

> I can muffle that window down. I take a blanket or some-thin' with me and put it over that window and hit it. And the only thing you can hear is that glass fallin' . . . Plop! Open the window up and go on in. (No. 009)

What is more, this strategy took less time than taping the window.

Despite precautions, the force required to break a window inevitably results in a certain amount of noise. And while the offenders accepted this, they had a clear idea about how much and what kind of noise was "safe," that is, unlikely to attract attention. Without exception, they believed that a single short, sharp sound was much safer than any sort of extended hammering or thumping. One subject, revealing considerable insight into human nature, explained: "Makin' one noise don't matter, but you can't be makin' two noises. People hear somethin' they gon say, 'What was that? You hear somethin'?' If they don't hear somethin' else, they ain't gon do nothin'." The offenders wanted to be sure to shatter the window with the first blow; in their eyes, the sound of each subsequent blow significantly increased the risk of being noticed. This meant that most of them did not try to overcome storm windows because doing so required the breaking of two or more panes of glass.

> [Storm windows are] supposed to have triple panes . . . You got to make too much noise to break three panes of windows. Now, one [pane] is no problem. (No. 037)

> Storm windows are hard . . . The only way you can get into those is if they are unlocked; I don't see no other way. (No. 025)

A few offenders responded to the threat of being heard while breaking into a target by not entering the place at once. They left the scene and hid nearby in case the sound had prompted someone to call the police. If, after a reasonable period of time, the police did not arrive, the offenders concluded that it was safe to carry on with the burglary.

> My friend went around the back and kicked in the basement door. Then that made a little noise so we went back down the street and made sure wasn't nobody up on what we was doin'. So we walked back down there [a little later] and we went in the house. (No. 043)

This same strategy sometimes was employed when offenders were worried about the presence of a burglar alarm. Because some alarms are silent, offenders frequently were reluctant to enter alarmed dwellings without waiting for some time after breaking in, even if no bell or siren had sounded.

> We stayed outside [the house] for about half an hour trying to figure out if [the alarm] was off or on so we figured we would break the window and find out. So the window was broke for about three hours and we sat across the road and just waited for something to happen. (Eddy Smith—No. 091)

> If I pop the door and see one of them burglar alarms on the window, I wait ten or fifteen minutes and see what happens; circle the block or something and then come back and see if the police done came. If the police ain't came, I know it's probably a fraud. (No. 066)

Most offenders, though, wanted to avoid alarms altogether and, upon encountering such devices, abandoned all thought of attacking the dwelling. Indeed, 56 of the 86 subjects we questioned about this issue said that they were not prepared to burglarize an alarmed residence under *any* circumstances (see Bennett and Wright, 1984).

Chapter 4

When I check the house out and be ready to get in it and I see an alarm, I'm all ready to bust a window and I see that, I'll just back off it. (No. 021)

I ain't never learned to deal with them alarms. I tried one before, you know, listening to somebody and they told me all you got to do is snip the wires from the alarm box. I did that and "dingalingaling." Man, he don't know what he was talking about. He gon have me in jail, you know. So you snip them alarms, they go off cause they got emergency back up on 'em. Just in case the power go off, they runnin' off a battery. Nah, I ain't never went in [a house with an alarm]. (No. 009)

I never mastered [disabling alarms]. I always thought I was slick and keen, but I never mastered that. I never learned how to unhook an alarm so if they had [one], I was out of there. (No. 099)

What is more, another eight offenders reported that they only attempted to tackle certain types of alarms, leaving others alone.

Some alarms you get around and some alarms you can't get around. Now they got what I call scary alarms, like those alarms when you walk up to it and it says, "Warning! Warning! You are in violation!" That's a scary alarm. That just deters you because it's a loud noise, you get on away from there. (No. 056)

Putting it another way, almost three out of four of the subjects in our sample were deterred by the presence of an alarm at least some of the time.

On the other hand, a quarter of the offenders we talked to about alarms claimed that they were not concerned about them. Only a few, though, had a sophisticated understanding of alarms and felt confident of their ability to disable them safely. Instead, most either believed that they could find a way around alarms by locating an unprotected access point or else simply did not care if they activated the devices because they would spend only a minute or two inside targets and knew that the police were unlikely to respond in time to apprehend them.

In effecting entry into an intended target, then, the offenders were endeavoring, first and foremost, not to draw attention to themselves. This typically required them to locate an access point that was reasonably well-protected from public view. Once a concealed place had been found, they next turned their attention to breaking into the dwelling. To do so, the offenders seldom employed anything more sophisticated than widely available objects such as screwdrivers, crowbars, hammers and masking tape. As noted in chapter 3, part of the attraction of residential burglary was that, generally speaking, it could be accomplished using only objects that anyone can obtain easily.

Handling the Fear of Legal Consequences

The actions described above form part of an essentially criminal undertaking and this means that offenders must carry them out under the threat of getting caught and punished. Those in our sample were not unmindful of this threat. Almost without exception, they acknowledged that all criminals, notwithstanding their level of skill, run some risk of arrest and prosecution. As one observed: "Even the best of plans and the best of timing can still get screwed up." While actually engaged in a burglary, the offenders employed various methods to mentally "handle" this prospect so that it would not interfere with their ability to offend. They consciously used techniques which allowed them to "neutralize" the capacity of threatened sanctions to deter an intended offense (Bennett and Wright, 1984). The most common involved a steadfast refusal to dwell on the possibility of being apprehended which, of course, precluded consideration of the contingent risks of prosecution and punishment (Bennett and Wright, 1984; Shover and Honaker, 1992; Tunnell, 1992). Two out of every three offenders we spoke to about this matter—67 of 101—reported that during offenses they typically tried to avoid thinking about the chance of getting caught.

> I try not to [think about the possibility of being apprehended]. I mean, I already know there's a chance of getting caught, so when you doin' something like that, you try and keep that off your mind. (No. 043)

> If [I thought about getting caught], I might not do it. If I get a little hunch and say, "Hmm, I might get caught if I do this," then I won't do it. So I try not to even think like that. (No. 038)

Some of the offenders seemed to find it easy to keep such thoughts out of their minds. In fact, a few of them denied considering the risk of apprehension altogether.

> When you lay down at night and you say, "I'm a do a burglary in the morning," the thought of gettin' busted and things is not there, it's just not there! You don't even think about it. When you get up and you gettin' ready to do it, ain't no thought of gettin' busted. If the thought was there and you constantly thinkin' about gettin' busted, you better not do it. (No. 055)

Most, however, had to work to stop themselves from contemplating the possibility of getting caught. These offenders had to "push" an awareness of that risk out of their minds.

> I be shakin' when I'm [doing a burglary] cause, you know, I have a feelin' that I'll get caught. But I'm tryin' not to think about that and have faith in what I'm doin'. (No. 047)

> I don't think about getting caught, but it's always in your head. But I don't think about it. You know, that [thought is] always there, but you don't let it discourage you . . . You know, I don't think about it, but it's there. You know what I mean? (No. 016)

That's always there, that thought [of being apprehended],
but you push it back so you can get on with what you got to
do. (No. 018)

Several of the subjects used alcohol or drugs prior to offending
as a means of dulling their concerns about being apprehended.
One, for example, explained his reasons for "getting high" before committing burglaries in the following terms: "[Drugs
make me] mellow. It's just like, 'I'm going to go in, do it, and
back out.' I don't think about all the [bad] things that could
happen to me." These burglars drank alcohol or took drugs in
a deliberate attempt to thwart the deterrence potential of official penalties and thereby facilitate their ability to offend.

Beyond a desire to weaken the deterrent effect of threatened
sanctions, a number of the offenders wanted to avoid thinking
about the chance of getting caught for other reasons. Some
felt that dwelling on this matter only served to create anxiety,
which impaired concentration and increased the probability
of making a mistake. From their perspective, thinking about
getting caught could actually be counterproductive (Bennett
and Wright, 1984).

[The risk of being apprehended] crosses my mind, but then I
just kind of block it out. You start thinking about that and
you start getting paranoid and start getting clumsy and stu-
pid. (No. 095)

Nine times out of ten you gon think about [getting caught],
even if it's just for a second. But when you do [a burglary],
you don't want to go in with that type of thought in your
mind. If it pop in your mind, flick it out just as quick as it
pop in. Just like that. Because you don't want to go in with
that thought. If you go in with that thought, you gon get
caught . . . If you go in to rob a place and all while you in
there you thinkin' you gon get caught, all that time you takin' on them thoughts ain't gon do nothing but mess you up
and get you caught. (No. 033)

Other offenders were superstitious and believed that thinking about getting caught, in and of itself, could cause them to be apprehended. They referred to this process as "burning bread on yourself."

> Thieves got a thang they say [about getting caught], "If you think about thangs like that, you burnin' bread on yourself." So you don't think about it . . . Just go for it. (No. 011)

Several of the subjects found it difficult to speak about the risk of apprehension, fearing that such talk would jinx their future illegal activities. Similarly, Taylor (1985:10) has noted that the "professional villains" he studied in London were reticent to discuss the possibility of arrest and punishment, pointing out that among active offenders these matters are "about as likely a topic for extended conversation as lung cancer at Imperial Tobacco." In discussions with potential partners about an upcoming offense, members of our sample were loathe to mention the chance of being caught. To do so, they believed, risked conjuring up bad luck and alienating a potential ally. As one told us: "If you bring [getting caught] up, a lot of people ain't gon do the crime."

Some of the offenders also tried not to think about getting caught because such thoughts generated an uncomfortably high level of mental anguish. They believed that the best way to prevent this from happening was to forget about the risk and leave matters to fate (Bennett and Wright, 1984).

> If you're gonna get caught, you're gonna get caught. But worrying about it and thinking about it [will] only cloud up your head, you know. I really just put it out of my mind. (No. 100)

Given that virtually all of these offenders perceived themselves as being under pressure to act quickly *and* as having no lawful means of alleviating that pressure, this makes sense. Where no viable alternative to crime seems to exist, there clearly is little point in dwelling on the potentially negative consequences of offending. It should come as no surprise, then, to learn that the offenders usually preferred to ignore the

possible risk and concentrate instead on the anticipated reward (see Shover, 1991).

> Yeah, I be nervous and scared, but I just think about the
> money. [I don't think about getting caught], just about the
> money. (No. 103)

Bluntly put, in many cases the offenders effectively had no
choice (Shover and Honaker, 1990); committing a burglary
was their only realistic option. In light of this fact, they chose
to think positively rather than negatively about the outcome
of their actions.

One third of the offenders in our sample, however, said that
they usually *did* think about the possibility of being apprehended during their residential burglaries. It is reasonable to
ask why a conscious awareness of this risk did not prevent
them from offending. Undoubtedly, the main reason can be
linked to the monetary return they expected, which, in practice, tended to overwhelm their concern about the potential
risk (Shover, 1991).

> I always think about the chances of getting caught, every
> time I do one. I try to tell myself that maybe the money I
> get might can offset the time I would get if I get caught. I
> just try and bargain with myself . . . I mean, I don't want to
> get locked up and I can't afford to get locked up. But I weigh
> that against that I need some money. [The money] always
> wins out. (No. 030)

By and large, the offenders perceived the chance of being apprehended for any given break-in as extremely slim and, in the
face of the anticipated payoff, found it easy to discount this
threat (see Wilson and Abrahamse, 1992). One of them explained his thinking this way: "Well, a chance of getting
caught, that's what a person got to take [if he wants that
money]. He know he taking a chance on anything he do that's
illegal, but [it's] a slim chance." Remember that the offenders
almost invariably knew something about intended targets
prior to committing their burglaries. This often provided them

not only with a reasonable basis on which to assess the risks involved in offending, but also with some information about the likely magnitude of the monetary reward. In other words, their "criminal calculus" (Shover and Honaker, 1990; Tunnell, 1992) was based on the best data available to them and, in that sense, should be regarded as "essentially realistic" (Bennett and Wright, 1984:118).

Other offenders who, while committing their burglaries, typically thought about getting caught felt that this awareness acted as a focussing force that led them to be especially careful. Being attuned to the risk of arrest, they believed, was beneficial; it served to concentrate their minds on the importance of avoiding detection.

> "Watch out or you will get caught!" That's how [the thought of getting caught] clicks in my head. You know, "Watch yourself or you will get busted." (No. 010)

Still other offenders simply accepted the fact that they might be apprehended, adopting a fatalistic attitude.

> I think about it, [but] if you get caught, you get caught. (Dan Ford—No. 101)

These subjects clearly were cognizant that they *could* get caught, but felt that whether this happened was a matter of fate and largely beyond their control. As they saw it, all one could do was to hope for the best. While this may seem irrational, it must be recognized that many people cope with perceived risks in this way. Those who smoke, for instance, typically do so in the full knowledge that this *might* damage their health. At the same time, though, they may well hope that their health will not suffer. The same may be said of crossing a street against the light or driving an automobile faster than is prudent.

Finally, there was one offender who thought about the possibility of apprehension while committing her burglaries, but nevertheless carried on because she was not overly concerned. She fully expected to be apprehended "sooner or later" and to receive a lengthy prison sentence. Yet, she remained indifferent to threatened sanctions.

> [I] think about gettin' caught. In a way I really don't care
> though. I mean I care a little, but it don't bother me that
> much . . . I care because I want to see my baby. If I go get in
> the penitentiary, I won't see her that much . . . In a way I do
> [care] and in a way I don't . . . I know one day I'm a get
> caught, so sometimes it really don't make no difference. (Yolanda Williams — No. 039)

In short, the offenders knew that, in committing burglaries, they risked being caught and punished. Most of them were able to push this thought out of their minds while engaged in an offense, thereby displaying a remarkable ability to undermine "the legal bind of the law" (Bennett and Wright, 1984:116). No doubt, this ability was facilitated by the fact that typically they were in a state of pressing need at the time. As Lofland (1969:50) has observed, all people in this situation have a tendency toward "psychosocial encapsulation" wherein they enter a "qualitatively different state of mind" in which the potentially negative consequences of their actions become attenuated (see, e.g., Cressey, 1953). Indeed, many of the offenders who, during their burglaries, *did* think about getting caught often were driven by financial pressure to discount that risk in the face of the expected payoff; a process made easier by a widely shared perception that the odds were in their favor. Much of the research on offender decision making fails to account for the role of motivation, that is, "the purpose and the meaning of a prospective criminal act," in modifying perceptions of risk (Shover, 1991:103). This is a serious omission because, in practice, the reason for contemplating a crime in the first place frequently serves to diminish the perceived threat of official sanctions (Lofland, 1969; Shover, 1991).

Handling the Guilt

The fear of legal consequences is not the only psychological mechanism that could dissuade would-be residential burglars from committing an offense. Burglary, after all, is widely regarded as morally reprehensible and, consequently, an anticipation of feelings of guilt also might constrain the activities of potential offenders. Certainly, all of the offenders knew that breaking into dwellings was wrong. As one said: "Our parents raised us on the Bible and all these wonderful things, [just like yours did]." However, the vast majority of those who commented on the morality of residential burglary — 83 of 99 — said they typically experienced little or no guilt when actually carrying out an offense.

> I don't feel guilty about [committing burglaries]. Shit, if I felt guilty about it, shit, then I wouldn't do it. (No. 016)

> I really don't feel guilty when I'm doing [a burglary]. (No. 056)

These subjects gave little or no indication of needing to "neutralize" feelings of guilt in order to offend (Sykes and Matza, 1957).

> I told you, I ain't got no conscience! What's a conscience? Somebody talk to your insides or something? (No. 022)

> [Guilt] just didn't bother me. (Money — No. 097)

Some contended that they *never* had been troubled by guilt while committing their burglaries.

> Nah, I don't feel guilty, man. Never! Never have I felt guilty about takin' nothin' from nobody. Never! (No. 011)

Others claimed that through repeated offending they had become immune to pangs of conscience.

> [I don't feel any guilt], none at all. It's like an everyday thang when you get used to it . . . Like me and you together and we beat [the project fieldworker] up in the wheelchair. That will make you feel real bad and low like, you know. But it won't bother me cause I done been through it before, done did it before. (No. 009)

For our purposes the important point is that during their offenses these subjects could not be constrained by a guilty conscience; they simply did not have one. A number of them, however, reported experiencing feelings of guilt at other times, especially immediately after completing a break-in. Those feelings, though, had a tendency to dissipate quickly so that, when the need to commit another residential burglary arose, they no longer carried any emotional force for the offenders.

> I mean, I felt guilty after I came out [of the house]. Then I thought about it and said, "Well, I done did it now. What's to worry about?" So I just put it out my mind and just went on. Eventually [the guilt] just went away; I started going into other houses. (No. 040)

Indeed, just one offender in our sample still seemed bothered by his most recent offense. But even he was quick to downplay the seriousness of his actions. He argued that burglary was not as bad as some other crimes and that victims often welcomed a break-in as providing an opportunity to replace worn out possessions.

> As far as that drug [selling] is concerned, they need to line everybody up against the wall and shoot them. That's my opinion. Cause that's destroyin' . . . the community . . . Now a burglary—which is wrong too, I know all wrong is wrong and right is right—but a burglary, in my opinion, they can go back and replace this and maybe get a better make than what they had. I mean they might say, "I'm glad they took the damn stereo. It was about ready to go out of style anyway. I wish they would have took the remote control that came with it. Then I can get me a bigger one." (No. 018)

On the other hand, 16 of the 99 offenders who addressed the issue of guilt said they usually did have pangs of conscience during their crimes. Given their need for immediate cash, however, the guilt experienced was not powerful enough to prevent them from offending.

I feel [burglary] is wrong. Some people work hard to buy their valuable things and a person like me who just happens to come take them, I do feel a little sympathy or whatever. But I need the money now! (No. 049)

I mean I feel guilty about [the burglary] . . . but you gotta do what you gotta do to survive. (No. 095)

The offenders in this group felt that, under certain circumstances, they had little choice but to commit a residential burglary and thus were able to do so despite their moral reservations.

In general, then, feelings of guilt were in short supply among the offenders we interviewed, with approximately five in six stating that their consciences did not bother them at all during offenses. Almost without exception, though, the subjects said that they knew burglary was wrong. Nevertheless, they typically did not pause to consider the moral implications of their actions while actually thinking about committing an offense. This, in turn, facilitated the initial decision to do a residential burglary by enhancing its "subjective availability" (Lofland, 1969:84). After all, other things being equal, most people are unwilling to engage in activities which they *consciously* consider to be morally repugnant. In the real world, of course, other things are not always equal and this explains how those offenders who usually *did* feel guilty came to commit their crimes; their moral qualms were overpowered by situational pressures, most notably the need to get money quickly.

Summary

By embarking on the task of actually breaking into their chosen targets, the offenders were exposing themselves to real risks. Realizing this, they typically became increasingly tense and agitated as they moved forward, wanting to put the offense behind them as quickly as possible. In such a state, the offenders had to approach would-be targets, make a last-minute check for occupancy, and effect an entry. This required them to maintain a firm grip on their emotions because outward signs of nervousness could attract suspicion from potential onlookers.

In approaching intended targets, most of the offenders attempted to project a "conventional appearance" (Katz, 1988). Generally speaking, they did this by using the simplest of tactics; a majority of them approached targets dressed as they were, perhaps armed with a plausible-sounding reason for being on the property in the event that someone should challenge them. Similarly, the offenders usually employed nothing more than everyday know-how to make a final check for occupancy; they knocked on the door, rang the bell, or called from a nearby telephone booth. The process of actually getting into the dwellings seldom required the offenders to possess highly specialized knowledge or sophisticated equipment. Most break-ins were accomplished by using common household tools to shatter a window, defeat a lock, or pry open a door. The technical simplicity of residential burglary almost surely was one of its principal attractions for the offenders in the first place.

The offenders had to carry out their burglaries under the threat of being apprehended and punished. During their crimes most of them consciously refused to dwell on the possibility of getting caught. In this way, they robbed the threatened sanctions of their deterrence value and thus could offend unimpeded by concerns about the potentially negative consequences. Some of the offenders *did* think about the risk of being apprehended, but still managed to proceed. By and large, they were able to do this because the anticipated reward overwhelmed their fear of getting caught. Again, it must be emphasized that these subjects most commonly were contemplating their offenses in response to financial pressure. The perceived attractiveness of the expected payoff was bound to be enhanced in such circumstances (Shover, 1991). Add to this the fact that the offenders knew the chance of being arrested for any given residential burglary was low and it is easy to appreciate how the weighing of risks and rewards resulted in a decision to offend.

Although all of the offenders clearly knew that residential burglary was widely regarded as being morally wrong, few experienced any guilt while committing their offenses. Those who did have moral qualms typically felt they had little choice but to offend, guilty conscience notwithstanding. In either case, the end result was that at the time of actually contemplating their crimes the subjects could not realistically have been dissuaded from offending by internalized moral beliefs.

The offenders did not view themselves as having the luxury of freedom of choice in committing their burglaries. Rather, they saw their decisions to offend as emanating from a desperate need—financial or otherwise—that could not easily be met through more conventional means. In a sense, the pressure of their immediate situation attenuated the perceptual link between offending and the risk of incurring sanctions; they entered a state of "encapsulation" (Lofland, 1969:50–54) in which *all* that mattered was dealing with the present crisis. We will elaborate on this phenomenon in chapter 7.

5

Search and
Departure Strategies

IN MOST JURISDICTIONS, a residential burglary has been completed in the eyes of the law the moment an offender enters a dwelling without permission, intending to commit a crime therein. But seen through the eyes of the burglars themselves, a break-in is far from complete at this point. Indeed, the offense has just begun. They must still transform their illicit intentions into action—which, in practice, almost invariably involves searching for goods and stealing them—and escape from the scene without getting caught, injured, or killed. In doing this, however, offenders are on the horns of a dilemma. On the one hand, the more time they spend searching a residence, the better chance they stand of "scoring big," that is, realizing a large financial reward. On the other hand, the longer they remain inside a target, the greater risk they run of being discovered. Having entered a dwelling, then, offenders must strike a deceptively complex, subjective balance that maximizes reward within the limits of acceptable risk. How is such a balance actually struck? The present chapter will seek to answer that question. Criminologists interested in the decision making of residential burglars have devoted almost no attention to this process, despite the fact that such offenders obviously continue to make decisions throughout the commission of their crimes. An examination of this matter, therefore, is crucial to the development of a fuller understanding of the decision-making calculus of property offenders.

Once inside a target, the first concern of most offenders is to reassure themselves, yet again, that no one is at home. They do this in a variety of ways. Some run through the dwelling and take a quick glance into every room. Others remain still and silent, listening for any sound of movement. Still others call out something along the lines of "Is anybody home?" More than anything, such actions probably represent an attempt by offenders to put worries about being attacked by an occupant behind them so that they can devote their attention to searching for cash and goods.

> When you first get inside, you go through all the rooms to make sure no one's home. Once [you see] there's no one home, that's when you start gettin' busy, doin' your job. (No. 014)

Thus having reassured themselves, offenders often experience a sudden realization that everything inside the residence is theirs for the taking. One of the female offenders in our sample said this realization made her feel as if she was in Disneyland, calling to mind a magical world in which fantasy had become reality. Another offender likened the feeling he got inside an unoccupied dwelling to being in a fashionable shopping mall, "except you don't have to pay for stuff; just take it." Comments such as these suggest that, during this phase of the burglary process, offenders perceive themselves to be operating in a world that is qualitatively different from the one they inhabit day to day. Katz (1988:56) refers to this world as "an enchanted land," the phenomenological creation of a mind bent on crime; it allows the offender to proceed, bolstered by "the recognition that the situation is miraculously constituted perfectly for the emergent [offense]."

Shielded from public view inside targets, many offenders also experience a marked reduction in anxiety. The actual break-in is behind them, there is no turning back, and it makes little sense to agonize over the potentially negative consequences of their actions. Recognizing this, offenders have a tendency to settle down, turning their attention to the task of searching the residence. Many of the subjects we interviewed reported that this was the case for them, some adding that, in settling down, they were able to search dwellings more effectively.

> Basically, you just calm down as you get in and notice no one's at home. When you calm, your brain functions and you can think. (No. 010)

This is not to suggest that the subjects stopped worrying about the risks altogether. Most of them continued to be somewhat fearful, with the length of time they were willing to spend inside targets providing a rough indication of the gravity of their concern. As one interviewee put it: "First thing I do is check to see if anybody there and then I'm just gettin' the merchandise. I don't want to be there too long." Not surprisingly, the amount of time that the offenders felt was safe to remain in dwellings often had a strong influence on the thoroughness with which they searched them. In broad terms, they typically employed one of two strategies in order to locate goods to steal: (1) the brief search; or (2) the leisurely search.

The Brief Search

The outside world does not stand still while offenders are burglarizing targets, and, as noted above, the offenders' vulnerability to discovery increases the longer they remain inside them. Occupants may return unexpectedly. Neighbors may become suspicious and call the police. Patrolling officers may spot something out of the ordinary (e.g., a broken window) and stop to investigate. Offenders are well aware of such risks and the vast majority of them respond by attempting to limit the time that they spend in dwellings. Certainly this was true for the burglars in our sample; 80 of the 86 offenders whose typical approach to searching houses could be determined—93 percent—said that they did not want to linger inside targets, preferring to get out as quickly as possible.

> When you first get in [to a dwelling], do whatever you gon do; do it quick and get on out of there! (No. 057)

> When you doin' [a burglary], you work fast. You go straight to what you want to get and then you come out of there. (No. 067)

> I know three minutes don't seem like a long time, but in a house that's long! You just go straight and do what you got to do; [three minutes is] a long time. (No. 050)

Here again, the ability of the offenders to locate goods without undue delay was facilitated by continued adherence to a cognitive script that guided their actions almost automatically as they proceeded through dwellings; this script helped them to flow through the search process without periodically having to stop to calculate their next move. Virtually all of the burglars we interviewed reported having a tried-and-true method of searching residences which, they believed, produced the maximum yield in cash and goods per unit of time invested. The search pattern varied somewhat from offender to offender, largely as a function of the time a given individual was prepared to remain inside a given target. With few exceptions, however, the interviewees were agreed that, upon entering a dwelling, one should make a beeline for the master bedroom; this is where cash, jewelry, and guns are most likely to be found. These items are highly prized by burglars, being light to carry, easily concealed, and representing excellent "pound for pound" value.

I'm hittin' that bedroom first. I'd rather hit that bedroom than the living room cause it's more valuables in the bedroom than it is in the living room—jewelry, guns, and money. So everything is in the back [of the dwelling] somewhere; most likely in the bedroom. (No. 009)

First I went in the bedroom and see if I could find some money. That's the first thing I usually do is go to the master bedroom . . . The master bedroom, that's the first place . . . I know that's where the valuable stuff is at. (No. 069)

The first thing you always do when you get to a house is you always go to the bedroom. That's your first move . . . [b]ecause that's where the majority of people keep they stuff like jewelry or cash. You know it's gon be a jewelry box in the bedroom; you know you ain't gon find it in the living room. Guns, you ain't gon find that too much in the living room. (No. 055)

The offenders believed that searching the master bedroom first also enhanced their personal safety, especially when this room was located on the second floor of a dwelling. A number of the subjects commented that they felt particularly vulnerable upstairs because their only escape route—the stairway—could easily be cut off should an occupant return unexpectedly. As a result, most of them wanted to begin their search on the second floor and get downstairs as quickly as possible in the belief that the odds of being discovered increased with the passage of time. (Indeed, a few confined their offending to "ranch style" or single story residences exclusively, such was their fear of being trapped upstairs.)

The offenders usually searched four places within the master bedroom. The first stop for most of them was the dresser, where they quickly went through each drawer—often dumping the contents onto the floor or bed—looking primarily for cash and jewelry.

[Y]ou got to look around, you got to ransack a little. You got to realize too that you don't have very much time to ransack neither . . . You always start in the bedrooms, in the drawers; that's where they keep the money and the jewelry. (No. 012)

The offenders typically went to the bedside table next, hoping to find a handgun and, perhaps, some cash and jewelry. From there, many of them turned to the bed itself in search of money; a number of our interviewees commented on the tendency of people, especially those who are elderly or poor, to keep their savings in or under the mattress. Lastly, the offenders usually rummaged through the bedroom closet. In doing so, they were looking mainly for cash and pistols. These items, they claimed, often were hidden in a shoebox or similar container placed alongside other boxes and containers in the closet.

Having searched the main bedroom with a modicum of success, some of the offenders did not bother to look through the remaining rooms, preferring simply to make good their escape. These subjects realized that a more exhaustive search of the premises could net them a larger financial return, but they were unwilling to assume the increased risk entailed in spending longer inside the target. As one offender who typically searched only the master bedroom explained: "You miss a lot, but it's all gravy if you get away." The majority of the offenders, however, conducted at least a cursory search of the rest of the dwelling before departing. A number of them said they usually had a quick look around the kitchen. Surprisingly, most of these subjects were not searching for silverware or kitchen appliances so much as for cash and jewelry; they claimed that such items sometimes could be found hidden in a cookie jar or in the refrigerator/freezer.

[The valuables are located in] either the freezer, the icebox, in they bedroom . . . in the dresser drawer or under the mattress . . . People put money in plastic bags behind the meat in they freezer. (No. 022)

Some of the offenders also searched the bathroom, concentrating on the medicine cabinet where they hoped to find not only psychoactive prescription drugs (e.g., valium), but perhaps hidden money and valuables as well.

> Like a lot of times I've [gone through] the medicine cabinets, quite a few people leave money in the medicine cabinet. I don't know if you've ever heard of that, but I . . . found about forty dollars in there once and the second time I found about twenty-five dollars. (No. 010)

Few subjects, however, bothered to rummage about in bedrooms occupied by young children because, in their view, such rooms were unlikely to contain anything worth stealing.

> I ain't gon even worry about the kids' bedrooms. Mom and Dad have all the jewelry and stuff in they room. I know the little kids ain't got nothing in they room. (No. 065)

> Little kids' rooms, I don't usually go in there because they don't usually have much. I don't have any kids so ain't no sense me goin' in there unless one of my little nieces or nephews might want something and I might keep an eye out for them. (No. 066)

Most of the offenders usually searched the living room just prior to leaving the target because the items kept there tended to be heavy or bulky (e.g., television sets, videocassette recorders, stereo units); hence they were best left to the last minute. Indeed, some offenders did not bother to search the living room at all; they believed that trying to exit targets carrying cumbersome living room items simply was too risky. One offender, for example, told us: "I don't carry no TVs . . . because that's an easy bust." And another added: "You never take nothing big. You look for [something small]; something won't nobody see you bringin' out."

By employing such strategies to search dwellings, the offenders usually could locate enough cash and other valuables to meet their immediate needs in a matter of minutes. As one of them said: "You'd be surprised how fast a man can go through your house." Occasionally, however, the predetermined search strategies used by the offenders failed to yield the expected results. This caused some of them to depart from their normal modus operandi, remaining in residences for longer than they felt was safe in order to find something of value.

> [I] go straight to the main spots where I think the main stuff is in. Never mess around with, well, at least try not to, stay out the petty spots. Bathrooms, you know, what you goin' in there for? I may go in there if the house ain't no good, you know, [isn't] what I thought it was; then I start gettin' desperate and stuff and lookin' everywhere. Gotta get somethin'. Let me see if they got a gold toothbrush, you know, just anything. (No. 066)

In breaking into the dwellings, these offenders already had assumed considerable risk and they were determined to locate something worth stealing, if only to justify having taken that risk in the first place. Add to this the fact that most of them were under pressure to obtain money quickly, and their decision to carry on searching despite the increasing risk of discovery seems more sensible still; to abandon the offense would require quickly finding and breaking into an alternative target, with all of the attendant hazards.

On other occasions, offenders were tempted to linger in residences owing to the discovery of something which convinced them that a desirable item must be located elsewhere in the building. Putting it differently, they were enticed into accepting a higher level of risk, believing that the extra time devoted to searching was justified by the potential reward.

> Then when I'm goin' through the dresser drawer or somethin', I might find shell boxes; they got a gun! Definitely! And I'm gon find it. (No. 009)

It is at this point that we can begin to glimpse the danger of allowing oneself to be seduced by the possibility of realizing a large financial gain. As noted above, the offenders are operating in a world that is qualitatively different from the one they otherwise inhabit, a world in which they can take whatever catches their fancy. It is easy to see how they could get carried away by the project at hand, trying to take everything and disregarding the risks altogether. Generally speaking, the offenders tried their best to avoid this threat by focussing on the items they originally had intended to steal, resolving not to get "greedy" by attempting to take anything beyond that.

> [M]ost of the time you want to get in and get out as quick as possible. See, that's how a lot of people get caught; they get greedy. You go in and get what you first made up your mind to get. When you take the time to ramble for other things, and look through this and look through that, you taking a chance. (No. 023)

> I put my mind on one thing. That's what I'm a get. I ain't gon be ransackin' all through there . . . See, I don't get greedy once I go in and do a burglary. (No. 046)

From the perspective of these subjects, it made little sense to risk stealing more than was necessary to meet their immediate needs. What is more, many of them would not be able to transport much of what they might be tempted to steal. As one put it: "I don't want to be in [the dwelling] that long. I ain't gon be able to carry all that stuff anyway."

Not surprisingly, we did encounter offenders who reported being seduced by the allure of the available goods such that they forgot all about the risks of lingering in the target.

> The stuff that was in there, it just had this attraction to your eyes. It made you feel like, "God, I need that!" you know. So that's what, so we just kept on . . . everything just attracted our eyes. (No. 103)

One member of our sample claimed that in her experience this was especially likely to happen to female offenders because they were "nosier" than their male counterparts.

> The guys don't go in and root through shit. They go in for the big shit and they're out! The girls are stupid enough to

stay there. Like me, I just got this wild hair up my ass to get
[the] credit cards . . . The girls get to be nosey like, if there
is a kid [living] there, like a girl, clothes, jewelry or something that the girl's got [in her room]. (Candy Johnson —
No. 093)

In the course of our research, however, we uncovered little
evidence in support of the claim that female offenders were
more vulnerable than males to getting carried away by the burglary project. Indeed, the clearest example of being seduced by
a dwelling well stocked with "good stuff" was provided by a
male burglar. This offender described a residential break-in
during which he had become all but paralyzed by the sheer
volume of goods available to him, unable to decide what to
take and what to leave behind. Only at the insistence of his
partner was he able to overcome his indecision and complete
the offense.

I was downstairs just lookin' around cause I was real choicy;
I was real choicy this last job I had. [My partner] came downstairs and said, "Man, you better get what you gon get and
come on!" "Man, what time is it?" I said, "I got about fifteen
minutes." He said, "Man, you better hurry up!" You know,
he was rushin' me then cause usually I be rushin' them. "Al-
right then, I'm a take this VCR, this TV, let's go." (No. 047)

Cases such as this, though, were the exception rather than the
rule; all of the burglars we spoke to *usually* stuck to a well-
rehearsed cognitive script in searching targets. Admittedly, a
few of them did not always enter dwellings intending to steal
specific items, sometimes preferring to allow themselves to be
seduced by whatever caught their eye. But even these offenders typically adhered to a set pattern in moving through residences.

When you go in [to a target], the first thing you do is go
straight to the back. As you go to the back, you already
lookin'. While you lookin', you pick certain things out that
you gon take with you that you know you can get. You can

pick them out just by lookin' as you walkin'. Then, when you turn around to come out of there, you already know what you gon get . . . It depends on what I spot and if I think it's of value; not no particular things. (No. 033)

Remember that the overwhelming majority of the offenders were acting to remove as quickly as possible what they perceived as intense financial pressure. Given the circumstances, they were not favorably disposed toward experimentation (Lofland, 1969); they simply wanted to steal enough to alleviate their current distress and escape without delay.

Many residential burglars, of course, commit their offenses acting in concert with others. Of the 85 subjects in our sample who were asked about co-offending, 59 (69 percent) said they always or usually worked with others, and another 8 (9 percent) told us they occasionally did so. That is, over three-quarters of those we interviewed reported committing at least some of their break-ins in the company of others. As Shover (1991:89) has observed, co-offending appeals to many burglars because "it facilitates management of the diverse practical demands of stealing." Foremost among these demands is avoiding detection; 20 of the 67 offenders who told us they worked with others—30 percent—said that doing so allowed them to locate and transport goods more quickly, thereby reducing the risk of being caught in the act.

[I have searched dwellings more extensively], but that was only when I do it with friends. Cause I have more time; while I'm downstairs, he's upstairs. It's all timing. Fast as you do it and then get out of there. (No. 021)

I guess [I work with others] because it would take so much time for me to have to look for everything all by myself. If it's two or three of us it will be that much quicker. (No. 007)

A lot of times the places that I normally pick, it's quite a few items there . . . But then I use someone else so we can get the job done and move on out; get away as soon as possi-

ble instead of making a lot of trips to get everything [out of
the dwelling]. (No. 040)

[I commit burglaries with a partner] just in case they have
lots of stuff in there I want. We can hurry up an' get it out.
(Carlion Jackson — No. 001)

A number of the offenders also reported that working with one
or more accomplices was safer than operating alone because it
permitted them to post a lookout.

It's always good to go in a house with at least three dudes.
You know, two of you'll get the stuff together. The other
one look out the window; he be the watch. (No. 011)

[I]t's almost always a little safer to have someone else with
you . . . Because if you got someone outside, they can always
give a little signal and let you know when someone's coming or whatever. If you're alone, you can't hear these things.
(No. 023)

These offenders believed that using a lookout not only was
objectively safer, it also carried the subjective benefit of elimi-
nating concerns about being caught by surprise and thus enhanced their ability to concentrate on searching for goods to
steal. As one of them noted: "By yourself, you never know
who behind you."

In a similar vein, some offenders who did not post a formal
lookout said that working with others gave them a sense of
security because the extra eyes and ears increased their capacity to detect signs of danger.

I figure it's a little more safer workin' with others . . . If both
of us got our minds and ears open [it's] safer. And it's
quicker, you know. (No. 052)

Moreover, several offenders pointed out that the presence of
accomplices represented ready assistance should they be attacked or encounter unanticipated resistance.

Sometime you want somebody with you . . . Sometimes I like to do [residential burglaries] with someone because I like to have protection in case something do happen. (No. 038)

[I work with someone else] because we spent five and a half years together and we can handle ourselves real well. I can trust him; if I get in a tough situation, he would kick ass for me. If a guy with a big baseball bat is going to come kill me, he'll come to the rescue type of thing. (No. 081)

A few offenders chose to work with others in the belief that this would increase the odds of at least one of them getting away should the police arrive unexpectedly.

[Working with others decreases the risk] because if it's more than one [offender] and the police do come, then somebody is bound to get away. (Christopher White – No. 005)

I guess if you get caught, you know, [the police] gonna catch one of yas, to put it that way, if you're gonna get caught, they're gonna catch one of ya, one of yas always gotta chance of getting away. (No. 092)

The logic underlying this belief was that two or more offenders could split up, running in different directions so that officers had to decide whom to chase and whom to allow to escape. Without exception, those we spoke to were in little doubt that they would be the ones to get away. The delusional aspect of this position is self-evident; why should the police elect not to pursue these offenders in favor of catching their accomplices? Here again, we are confronting a force that transcends rationality. The offenders acknowledged the risk of apprehension but believed that, because luck was on their side, they personally would avoid such a fate. That said, it remains true that by working with others, offenders may well reduce their individual risk of being caught during a police chase. One subject referred specifically to this fact: "I work with some partners because it's a better chance of gettin' away. They might get caught and you might get away." Along the same lines, another burglar told us that he liked working with others because witnesses have a tendency to confuse the features of multiple offenders, making it difficult for them to provide the police with a good description of individual suspects. In effect, this subject felt that the mere presence of co-offenders lessened the chances of getting caught should someone happen to witness a burglary in progress.

Quite a few of the offenders who committed their break-ins with others reported doing so just in case they *did* get caught. Most of these subjects simply wanted the reassurance of knowing that, should they be arrested, their co-offenders would be there with them to share the guilt and shame (see Shover, 1991).

> [I work with others] cause I feel if I get caught, I want them to get caught with me. I mean, I don't want to get caught by myself . . . They gon get caught with me . . . I feel I won't be so guilty if I have somebody with me. Then I won't feel so guilty, I'll feel kind of safe. (No. 039)

Two experienced female offenders, however, did not want to *share* the blame with accomplices, but rather sought to shift it entirely onto their associates. Both of these offenders worked exclusively with men, believing that the police would be inclined to show leniency toward a woman who claimed that she had been coerced into an offense by her male partners.

> I think down in my mind, when I first started doing burglary I saw a show and in it the woman claimed mental incompetent; that she'd been brainwashed. And I guess I feel like if we ever got caught that I could blame it on him. That's a pretty shit attitude, but . . . I don't know, I kind of feel like I'm smarter than [the male burglars] are. (No. 100)

There may be a grain of truth in this belief (see Simon, 1975; Simon and Landis, 1991). Be that as it may, the important point for our purposes is that these women were convinced this was the case, and thus were able to mentally discount the threat of arrest and punishment. This allowed them to get on with the business of searching targets, unimpeded by concerns about getting caught.

In short, the offenders who chose to work with others in committing their residential burglaries did so not only for practical reasons but for psychological ones as well; the company of accomplices dampened the offenders' fear of arrest and bolstered their confidence (Shover, 1991). Many of them recognized this fact, making explicit reference to the process in the course of speaking to us.

> Like I told you, I know it sounds strange, but I be scared when I do [a residential burglary]. Then if I have somebody with me and they say, "Ah, you can do it," they boost me up and I go on and do it. (Karen Green—No. 061)

> [I work with someone else] when I don't really know about that place, you know, I'm kind of nervous about it. So I feel like I wouldn't be as nervous by me havin' somebody with me on a place that I don't know too much about. (No. 020)

A few went so far as to say that they were too frightened to commit a break-in on their own. As one observed: "I don't know [why I've never done a burglary by myself]; I just figure I'll get caught and don't do it."

While co-offending has a number of potential advantages, working with other criminals inevitably entails certain risks. In the best of circumstances, such individuals are of dubious reliability and the pressures inherent in offending can undermine their trustworthiness still further. As Shover (1985) has noted, the strain of dealing with unreliable accomplices is viewed by many offenders as one of the major drawbacks to a life of crime. Several of the burglars we interviewed said that they were becoming increasingly reluctant to work with others, having been let down in the past by co-offenders who failed to carry their weight during offenses.

> See, you can't depend on no one else. That's why I'm goin' to court now . . . I had this so-called buddy of mine supposed

to be watchin' this house for me [while I was inside]. And I told him to stand across the street so when I come out I can look across the street and see him. When I came out, he was gone and I had merchandise up under my arm. So I said, "Let me get on out of here." I don't know what happened, he might have just left me. So I was gettin' nervous and I just went on and left. And there the police was! Walked right into they arms! (No. 049)

Even those who continued to work with others typically believed that, should something go wrong, their crime partners might well let them down. Eleven of the offenders in our sample expressed concern about whether accomplices could undergo police interrogation without naming them as co-participants.

You never know, it just ain't no sure thing. I just say, "Do unto others what's done unto you." So I'm not banking on [my partner's ability to remain silent]; if he get caught, then maybe that's damn near my ass is probably caught too. Cause I know if the police say, "Was somebody with you?" he'll probably say, "Yeah, yeah, oh yes." Police talk to you, you know; [partners] start spillin' they guts. They scared and then all they thinkin' about is themselves. So to be truthful with you, yeah, I never bank on [silence]. (No. 066)

Surprisingly, most of these offenders appeared to accept the potential for duplicity among their colleagues with equanimity; the police put pressure on arrestees to inform on their partners and it was naive to expect them to remain silent. One put it this way: "[My co-offenders] would probably tell on me, but, to be honest, I'd probably tell on them too."

Other members of our sample identified additional problems attached to co-offending. For example, a burglar who usually committed offenses alone told us that accomplices could not be trusted to refrain from violence should an occupant surprise them during a break-in.

That's the whole point of goin' [on burglaries] by yourself. If
you have somebody else with you and they panic . . . , they
might hit somebody. Then you got an assault charge. Acci-
dentally kill somebody and then you both got a murder
charge. You might get an additional charge put on it that
you don't need if you get caught. (No. 044)

Another offender said that working with others was distract-
ing, keeping an eye on partners made it difficult to concentrate
on the job at hand.

It's better to go by yourself cause you will be able to concentrate and think more better. You don't need to worry about
where your partner's at or if he got caught. (No. 048)

Perhaps the aspect of co-offending that the burglars found
most irksome involved what they perceived as a tendency for
accomplices to "cuff," that is, neglect to tell them about, some
of the loot found during the search of a target. In their eyes, it
was bad enough having to split the proceeds of their crimes,
without having to confront the possibility that their coworkers would try to cheat them. Some offenders attempted to reduce the risk of being cheated by working only with those they
knew well. For a few, this strategy seemed to pay off.

Well, like they say, "There's no honor among thieves."
That's what they say, [but] I believe that they really are
wrong about that because this here is really loyal. We done
did one house, man, where this guy had [a pistol he found
during the search] in his pocket already and we didn't know.
But he came out and told us when we was splittin' everything up. He took it out and he put it with the rest of the
shit to be split up. I wouldn't a did it; I would've kept that.
(No. 024)

Nevertheless, most of them continued to believe that even
close acquaintances might try to deceive them by cuffing
booty.

That's why I work with the same people, you know what I mean? He don't know what I got from downstairs. I might have found a ten-thousand-dollar diamond ring. Of course, you got to trust these damn fools, you know? It's easy to do man; it's easy for somebody to rip you off. (No. 064)

One offender reported that he and his usual burglary partner had an agreement whereby they always searched the master bedroom together. The logic behind their agreement, he told us, rested on the fact that the most easily concealed valuables tended to be found in this room; going through it together represented a means of "keeping each other honest."

Despite the risks of co-offending, the majority of those we spoke to continued to work with others. As much as anything, their decision to do so undoubtedly reflects the powerful influence of routine. The burglars were used to co-offending. Many of them worked with regular partners, having developed cognitive scripts that incorporated roles for their accomplices. These roles were well understood by their co-offenders and therefore break-ins could be carried out efficiently, with a minimum of confusion or conflict.

I work with him because when you get a [regular] partner, it's like two pieces of a machine; two gears clicking together and that's the way me and him work. (No. 056)

Everybody has they routine. I check upstairs and then they stay downstairs and get the VCRs and everything. That's the routine we been doing for years. (No. 039)

When the pressures that gave rise to burglaries intensified, then, it made little sense for offenders to deviate from their typical modus operandi by setting off alone. As noted in chapter 2, these pressures often arose in the context of partying—a group activity—where a shared desire to obtain fast cash for more alcohol or drugs precipitated a decision among those present to commit an offense. A burglar in our sample explained his reason for working with others thusly: "We be gettin' high together anyway, I might as well go [with] them. I come back by myself, they gon get high with me anyway." Additionally, it must be remembered that these offenders, like most of the burglars who worked alone, wanted to get in and out of targets as quickly as possible; such a goal is not conducive to innovation and hence it is unsurprising that they continued to work with others. People are not receptive to change when they are in a hurry.

The Leisurely Search

On any given residential burglary, the safest course of action for offenders is to search the target quickly and then leave without delay. Adopting this approach, however, means that they seldom will come away from offenses having stolen more than is necessary to meet their immediate financial needs; there is unlikely to be anything left over to help them deal with their next monetary crisis. The price of reducing the risks in the short term by limiting oneself to a brief search, therefore, may well be a foreshortening of the time between break-ins and a consequent increase in the frequency with which those risks must be taken. Some burglars, albeit a small minority, are unwilling to pay this price, preferring instead to remain in targets long enough to make certain that they have found everything of value. Six of the offenders in our sample—7 percent of those whose search style could be ascertained—reported that they typically searched dwellings in a leisurely fashion because they wanted to locate and steal as much as possible before departing.

> [I take] the whole day going through the whole house, sitting down and eating and things of that nature . . . On a burglary, you get all that you can. Some people will just go get certain items, [but] I can just take everything cause everything has a value. (No. 085)

These offenders claimed to understand the schedules kept by the occupants of their targets and to have a clear idea about how long the residents would be out. Thus, they could proceed largely unimpeded by concerns about being discovered in the act of searching places.

> When I do a burglary, I don't go in there and come back out. I go in there and stay! I go in there and stay for a couple of hours. I know these people won't be back home until about five in the evening if they leave at seven in the morning. I be done ransacked the house by then. (No. 017)

Even offenders who did not routinely linger in targets occasionally succumbed to the temptation to stay longer when they knew that the occupants would be away for some time. Their reasons for doing so, however, often seemed to transcend the desire for greater financial rewards. Indeed, many devoted this extra time almost wholly to relaxation and entertainment.

> I usually go straight to the bedroom and then I walk around to the living room. [Then I leave right away.] I have set at people's house and cooked me some food, watched TV and played the stereo . . . I knew they wouldn't be there. But I usually go straight to the bedroom. (No. 057)

The offenders recognized that these offenses were special, being largely free of the temporal constraints that circumscribed most of their break-ins. They responded by taking full advantage of the situation and making themselves at home. In effect, they were acting out the widely held adolescent fantasy of having the run of a place without the obligation to answer to anyone. Some of them, of course, *were* adolescents. But even among those who were older, few had any experience of being in full control of their living space; the majority still lived with their mothers or had no fixed address, staying with a succession of lovers or with whomever else would have them. It is easy to appreciate why they enjoyed having someplace to themselves. The irony is that they seldom did anything very outrageous. Like teenagers left alone for the weekend by their parents, most simply helped themselves to whatever alcohol and food was available and took pleasure in not having to clean up afterward. One, for instance, told us: "Sometimes I cook me some breakfast, but I never wash the dishes." None of these offenders remained in residences in order to "trash" them, except where a burglary was motivated by the desire for revenge.

A number of the burglars we interviewed said that they sometimes urinated or defecated inside their targets. They attributed their need to do so to the emotional pressures involved in offending. Contrary to popular media accounts, however, they generally did not use the carpet for this purpose; most of them reported using the toilet, sometimes not flushing it afterward because the resulting noise could drown out the warning sounds of approaching danger. A couple of our respondents did admit to relieving themselves in rooms other than the bathroom, but they explained this action in terms of safety—they did not want to risk getting cornered, literally with their pants down, in a small space with just one exit— rather than attributing it to any special contempt for the residents (see Walsh, 1980b). At the same time, these respondents seemed untroubled about the distress that this might have caused their victims; their sole concern was for their own well-being.

In summary, just a few of the offenders made a habit of lingering in targets for the purpose of conducting an exhaustive search of the premises. They did so in the belief that the increased short-term risk had a long-term payoff; their chances of realizing a large financial gain were enhanced, thereby reducing the odds that they would have to commit another offense in the near future. Whether this strategy was objectively safer than the brief search cannot be determined from our data. Five of the six offenders who always searched extensively had been arrested for burglary in the past, and three had been convicted. But spending longer in each dwelling may have been a response to, rather than a reason for their previous lack of success. In any case, it is unsurprising that most of the offenders in our sample eschewed this method of operation. As noted above, they typically were under pressure and trying desperately to relieve that pressure. Under such circumstances, offenders are unlikely even to consider the potential long-term benefits of taking a short-term chance (Lofland, 1969). All that matters to them is dealing successfully with their immediate crisis.

Being Thrilled

Katz (1988:64) has called attention to the "euphoria of being thrilled" experienced by amateur thieves immediately upon exiting the scene of the crime. He attributes this euphoria not so much to the excitement of material acquisition as to the avoidance of the shame that would accompany apprehension.

> Success brings in its wake emotions that go far beyond the joy of material acquisition. The "it" in "getting away with it" is not just the object, but something significantly shameful. Thus, the other side of the euphoria felt from being successful is the humiliation from being caught. What the sneak thieves are avoiding, or getting away with by not being caught, is the shame they would feel if they were caught. (Katz, 1988:64–65)

Being thrilled, he asserts, is unique to amateurs because experienced thieves are likely to see themselves as criminals and to take the possibility of arrest in their stride, regarding it as an occupational hazard; thus, successfully avoiding such a fate—getting away with it—does not bring them the same sense of relief. This assertion, however, is open to challenge. While seasoned offenders may view the threat of apprehension as just another "cost of doing business" (Katz, 1988:66), it is simply untrue that this necessarily insulates them from the euphoria that follows a successful theft. A number of the burglars in our sample, including some with lengthy criminal records, described experiencing an intense feeling of elation once they had escaped from the target.

Sometimes [doing a burglary] is funny, sometimes it ain't. It ain't funny when you get caught. But, uh, it feels good, I'm a tell you, if you get it and get away with it. It feels good! More excitin' than 'Nam [and] Viet Nam was real excitin'. (No. 045)

Some of them laughed and joked about the break-in with their co-offenders or streetcorner peers.

[Right after a burglary], we might sit down and laugh and joke about it with the fellas: "We clean them out, dude! When they come home, I don't know how they gon watch bull cause we got the TV!" You know, sittin' and laughin' and joke about it. (No. 009)

After we did [the burglary] there was some conversation . . . It was like we were laughing and giggling — "Oh man, that was sweet!" — you know. (No. 069)

Others celebrated more privately, but no less intensely, laughing to themselves as they replayed the offense in their mind's eye.

You might not believe it, but every time I do a burglary I get in there and get to laughin'. I get *real* happy when I leave. I always turn around and look at the house . . . Yeah, I do [think about the fact that I could have been caught], I think of that. After I done the burglary or probably that night if I get high and I'm at home, I'm thinkin' about it. But I'm also thinkin', "I done got away!" And I get to laughin'. (No. 017)

I don't think [that I could have been caught] until after it's over. Then that's something to laugh about because you done got away. (No. 051)

Clearly, the experience of being thrilled for these seasoned criminals closely matched that of the amateur thieves described by Katz (1988:65) who "shuddered and shook in elation, often to rhythms of laughter" following the successful completion of an offense. How can we account for this similarity? It is unlikely that avoiding the shame of arrest, in and of itself, held as much emotional force for the experienced offenders who made up our sample as it did for the novices surveyed by Katz. After all, those we spoke to invariably defined themselves as active hustlers, identified with the criminal subculture and, with just a few exceptions, had one or more previous arrests. Such factors must have protected them somewhat from the shame that might accompany being identified publicly as a thief. This is not to suggest, however, that they were wholly immune to the threat of being shamed. Several of the offenders, for example, told us that they did not want their spouse, children, or parents to find out that they were committing residential burglaries. And recall that some of them reported working with others so as to be able to share the guilt and shame should they get caught. Perhaps a more important reason for their intense relief at escaping detection, though, is that, as experienced criminals, they almost certainly would have received a stiff sentence for the crime. Beyond having avoided this fate, the offenders had just removed the pressure, financial or otherwise, that caused them to offend in the first place. Is it any wonder that they were every bit as thrilled as their amateur counterparts?

Summary

The vast majority of offenders wanted to search targets as quickly as possible in the belief that the longer they remained inside, the more chance they stood of being discovered. They did this by adhering to a cognitive script developed through trial and error to assist them in locating the maximum amount of cash and goods per unit of time invested. Using this script, the burglars could proceed almost automatically, without having to make complicated decisions at each stage of the search process. Although the script varied from one offender to the next, it usually called for them to search the master bedroom first; this is where money, jewelry, and guns were most likely to be found. The living room typically was searched last because the items kept there tended to be difficult to carry and hence were best left until the last minute. Many of the burglars worked with others as a means of expediting the search process, which could take place in different parts of the residence simultaneously. By employing a consistent, well-rehearsed modus operandi in searching dwellings, the offenders usually could locate enough valuables to meet their immediate needs in a matter of minutes. Having successfully done so, they would leave without delay. As most of them were offending in the face of a perceived financial crisis, this makes perfect sense; able to deal with that crisis, they thus were anxious to hurry up and finish the job.

By the time an offender has entered a target with the intention to steal, a burglary has been committed; the offense can no longer be deterred or prevented. It is at this point that criminologists and crime prevention experts show a marked tendency to lose interest, ceding the field to victimologists and police investigators. This is unfortunate because the activities of offenders *during* break-ins also may have implications both for decision-making theory, especially in regard to deterrence, and for crime prevention policy. To be sure, the offenders have not been deterred by the threat of sanctions, but that threat nevertheless seems to have a pronounced effect on their actions as they search targets. Most are unwilling to remain inside for long, foregoing the possibility of greater rewards in favor of reducing the risk of being discovered. In fact, for actual offenders this may be where deterrence operates most effectively. And even after it is too late to prevent the burglaries, there are still opportunities to limit the loss of cash and goods if we can understand well enough, and thus disrupt, the cognitive scripts used by burglars to search dwellings rapidly and efficiently. These matters will be explored further in chapter 7.

6 *Disposing of the Goods*

THE FINAL HURDLE to be overcome in the commission of residential burglaries involves disposing of the property stolen. A few offenders manage to avoid this obstacle by never stealing anything other than money or items for personal use, but they are very much the exception. Most have to find a buyer for the "hot" property resulting from their break-ins. This can be a troublesome task, requiring offenders once again to balance risk and reward while under considerable emotional pressure in an environment full of possible hazards. By canvassing several potential customers before striking a deal, they might be able to obtain a better price for their goods. This approach, however, exposes them to additional risks; not only must they hold on to the property for longer, they also must let a greater number of people know that it is in their possession. Added to this quandary are the interactional difficulties inherent in the trading of any sort of "tarnished goods"

(Shover, 1975). Property known to be stolen carries both risk and stigma. This can complicate still further the process of selling it; some potential customers simply will not buy such property, while others are reluctant to pay more than a small percentage of its retail value. Thus, offenders may have a strong incentive to obscure the origin of the goods they are offering for sale. In disposing of the proceeds of their burglaries, then, offenders face a variety of challenges. How do they overcome these challenges? That is the question to be addressed in this chapter. The goal is to explore the decisions entailed in disposing of stolen goods within the larger context of committing a residential burglary, that is, to investigate the perceptual links between this process and other aspects of offender decision making.

No sooner have offenders exited from a target than the majority of them turn their thoughts to getting rid of the goods as quickly as possible. Certainly this was the case for most of the burglars in our sample.

Soon as I get the stuff and I'm out the house, I'm going straight to [my regular buyer]. He buys it off the bat. Once I get [the property], it won't be in my possession an hour. (No. 020)

If I break in a house, I'm just grabbing something light that I can turn over there and then. (No. 021)

When you committing a crime, you want to get rid of the merchandise as quick as you can. (Fast Black — No. 084)

Much of their hurry undoubtedly was due to a fear that the property could incriminate them in a police search.

If you go selling [stolen goods] to different people and stuff, you might have that thing for two or three days and get busted with it. So you don't want nothing on you like that. If a cop did come and get you, what have they got? (No. 083)

I just don't want no shit in my house, 'specially some shit that I might have to keep for a day or a day and a half or some shit like that. (No. 017)

Equally important, however, was the pressure of their immediate circumstances. Goods had to be converted into cash before the financial difficulties that typically motivated their residential burglaries could be dealt with.

I don't want to go through the hassle [of hawking the goods around to get the best price]. I want to get my drugs then, see? I go to [my usual buyer], get the money and then go on about my business. (No. 011)

I choose to do it that way; I choose to get rid of whatever I have the quickest way I can . . . so I can get my money. (No. 038)

We don't like to hold the stuff; get rid of it and go on and do our thing. We don't hold it . . . [We sell it and] go and buy some heroin and go out and party. (No. 043)

For the offenders we interviewed, the period following a break-in was characterized by mounting anticipation of relief from what they perceived as financial desperation. All they had to do was to sell the stolen property and their monetary woes would be a thing of the past. Despite their anxiousness to accomplish this task, however, they had to continue to exercise caution; attempting to sell goods to the wrong person could get them into serious trouble. A potential customer might go to the police or, worse yet, take matters into their own hands. As one burglar explained: "Somebody might say, 'Hey, that's mine!' I might get beat up or put in jail or whatever. I might end up dead!" Most of the offenders sought to minimize the possible dangers by dealing only with people they knew to be interested in buying the property. Further, they tried to approach only those they trusted to remain close-mouthed about who sold that property to them, or, alterna-

tively, they would avoid disclosing their names or other identifying information to would-be buyers. In practice, this
typically meant disposing of their stolen goods through one of
four avenues: (1) a professional fence; (2) a pawnshop; (3) a
drug dealer; or (4) a friend, acquaintance, or relative.

The Professional Fence

Contrary to popular belief, only a minority of residential
burglars use a "professional fence" — someone who, on a regular basis, knowingly purchases stolen property for resale — as a
primary outlet for proceeds of their break-ins. In a study of
police reports, for instance, Cromwell et al. (1991:73) found
that just 30 to 40 percent of the booty taken in solved burglaries was disposed of in this way, speculating that "the professional fence may have been displaced by a more diverse . . .
market for stolen property." Certainly the results of our research lend support to the assertion that burglars have numerous potential outlets for their hot goods, with only a small
proportion using the services of a professional fence; just 20 of
the 90 offenders for whom information was available (15 subjects either did not speak to this issue or else could not identify
a dominant personal sales technique) typically sold the property they stole to such a buyer. More than anything, this probably reflects the fact that many of the streetcorner hustlers in
our sample lacked sophisticated underworld connections.
Most of them did not know a professional fence and had little
idea of how to go about contacting one.

Having connections to the world of professional fencing is
one of the major distinctions between high-level burglars and
their lowlier counterparts (Shover, 1991). Not surprisingly,
such connections were valued greatly among the offenders in
our sample; compared to the available alternatives, disposing
of stolen goods through a fence offered several advantages. For
example, a number of well-connected burglars told us that
they typically went straight to a fence with the proceeds of
their break-ins because doing so saved them the trouble of go-

ing from place to place to find someone willing and able to buy the property.

> I sell [the goods I steal] to a fence . . . Then I don't have to do a whole lot of carryin' if I go to him. I know he got his money on hand. I don't have to hang on to [the hot goods] then. (No. 015)

> Why not [use a fence]? I mean, you got a pillow case full of stolen rifles and guns and phones, I mean, you can go to one guy and say, "Give me a thousand dollars man and keep this." Or, "Give me three hundred dollars." And if it's some good shit, you'll get three hundred dollars as opposed to me stealing it and then I got to come to you and sell it and then you sayin', "Nah, I don't know if I want it." (No. 019)

> [I go to a professional fence] because your fence is your best bet. Who else you gon sell a lot of merchandise to? . . . Nobody on the streets gon pay that much money for stuff. Got to have somebody that has some money. You can't sell that kind of stuff on the streets; you can't walk up to somebody and say, "Give me three hundred dollars for this diamond ring." They ain't got that kind of money. (No. 030)

According to these offenders, dealing with a fence was not only more convenient than selling their property through any other outlet, it was also far safer; it kept to a minimum the number of people they had to approach as potential customers while limiting the amount of time that the stolen merchandise had to remain in their possession. In addition, fences had a vested interest in secrecy—they too were vulnerable to arrest—and therefore were inclined to be discreet about their transactions (Shover, 1975).

> [I use fences because] they have the money and they gon cover up [the fact that the property is hot]. (No. 030)

> [I sell the property I steal to fences because] you ain't got to worry about nobody snitching on you and things like that. (No. 037)

[Our fence is] real quiet, he don't talk a lot. Cause some people they be sayin', "Well, these girls they doing this and that." And you can't let everybody know what you doing, so that's why we go to him. (No. 071)

Such discretion is crucial where offenders have committed a highly publicized burglary involving the theft of easily identifiable property. Should their names become linked to the burglary, word of mouth on the street would quickly bring them to the attention of the police. Thus, they have little option but to seek out the services of a fence. One of the burglars we interviewed, for instance, described breaking into the residence of a local celebrity and stealing several unusual pieces of valuable jewelry. She explained that all of the jewelry had been taken to a fence, adding, "We couldn't just sell it on the street; it was like too hot to handle."

Another advantage of dealing with professional fences mentioned by those in our sample who had used them was that they conducted transactions in a business-like manner, without asking questions about where property came from, how it was obtained, and so on. In this sense, fences facilitated such transactions by "treating [them] as perfectly normal and routine business, avoiding any definition that would arouse the [offenders'] concern" (Shover, 1975:485). Although none of the well-connected burglars said so specifically, it seemed to us that they also liked dealing with fences because there was no need to disguise the fact that their goods were stolen.

I just take [my stolen goods] to a fence. That's because I don't want to go through the changes . . . Fence don't ask you no questions either. (No. 011)

Yeah, he know when he see me comin' that I done did something. The first thing that come out of his mouth is, "What have you got now?" (No. 065)

[I take the property I steal to a fence] because then you don't got to dick around . . . You can just take it to them and get rid of it. "What have you got?" Show them and how much you want for it and they will give you a price and get rid of it. (No. 077)

As noted above, the offenders were likely to be anxious as they attempted to sell the proceeds of their break-ins, wanting to get rid of the property because it was hot and looking forward to securing the cash necessary to solve their current financial crisis. In such an agitated emotional state, they were bound to be attracted to the calm, matter-of-fact approach of the professional fence; the illicit nature of the transaction was taken for granted by the buyer and therefore the added stress of maintaining a facade of legality could be avoided. Some fences, however, tried to exploit the desire of offenders to conclude deals as quickly as possible by offering them a paltry sum for their stolen merchandise (see Shover, 1975). This was true especially in cases where a fence believed the seller to be chemically dependent — someone perhaps disinclined to hold out for a better price when offered enough cash to purchase that day's drug supply.

> Lots of times [the fence will] try and bargain you down; . . .
> "Oh, that's too much, man!" . . . See, they try and trick you.
> See, they know you a dope fiend. That's why they figure you
> out dealin', cause you dope fiendin'. (No. 011)

Sometimes offenders felt that they simply had to accept such offers.

> I know I don't [get a fair price when I sell to a fence], but
> then [the property] be somethin' like I don't want period. I
> be wantin' it, but a lot of people might not can use the
> fuckah and I know it's worth fifty and here this bastard
> comin' with twenty or fifteen. But hey, he can have it! I be
> done gave it to his ass anyway. (No. 016)

> Say you got a fifteen hundred dollar watch, [a fence] might
> give you five hundred dollars . . . for it. You don't never get
> half. You might get a third or sometimes a fourth! But what
> can you do if the shit is hot? Who else you gon sell it to?

You don't want to take no stolen shit home, you want to get rid of it. Whatever he give you for it, you gon take it. You rather take five hundred dollars from him because you know ain't nobody on the streets gon give you that much for it. And you don't want to take it home, so you just take whatever he can give you for it. (No. 030)

But offenders who knew more than one fence often were emboldened to try to negotiate a higher price, secure in the knowledge that alternative outlets were available to them.

If you are going to do [burglaries] all the time, you have to have a fence. You need more than just one too. If one won't give you the right price, what you want for it, you can go see three or four different ones. And they know that, so they are all going to give you a decent price and they are going to buy what they can. (No. 038)

In order to negotiate effectively with fences, the offenders had to know the black-market value of the goods they were attempting to sell. Most of them were well aware of the current street prices of the various items that typically made up their inventory and had a basic understanding of the market forces that accounted for those prices.

That's the deal with your fences; if you know who to sell to and what, you can get a good price out of it. Say I got ten lawn mowers and each one of them costed like two hundred and fifty or three hundred dollars apiece. I'm not going to sell all of them to that man for a high price. I'll take a hundred dollars apiece for them. That's a thousand dollars right there. He in turn is going to make seventy-five dollars off them at least, no less than fifty dollars off each one of them. So he is going to make his money back plus a profit . . . That's how they do it. Usually where there is a fence you got people coming in and buying. They got a place to put [stolen property] or they got people in mind that wants it already, so they got their stuff sold. They already know they got their money coming . . . Say I got ten lawn mowers that cost that much; he might say, "I'll give you seven hundred for all of them." Of course, I am going to take it. That's seven hundred dollars that came easy! That's seven hundred and I don't have to tote them around with me no more. Same thing with TVs, VCRs or anything like that. VCRs usually go for one hundred dollars. Now they are starting to come down a little bit. It depends on what kind it is, you can get a hundred and fifty if it's a real good brand. Most of them is a hundred, some of them seventy-five . . . For certain things that got prices on them like that you'll get certain prices for, some things you won't. For example, weed eaters, they cost about a hundred and fifty [retail]. The most you are going to get out of a weed eater is sixty dollars. Different things got different value to it. A tiller costs about the same as a lawn mower [retail, but] I can get a hundred and fifty easy out of a tiller that's new because every [burglar] don't go get those things. (No. 083)

A few of the less experienced offenders who dealt with fences, however, claimed to have little idea of what the goods they stole were worth. These offenders were poorly equipped to haggle over prices; thus, they tended to accept on faith whatever remuneration initially was offered.

I don't know shit about guns, but I know a gun dealer [who buys stolen pistols] that doesn't live far from me and I mean he's legit—owns a business and works out of his own house. And I just, "Here you go." I know I don't know nothing, but I know he's not gonna rip me off. (No. 095)

Even the more seasoned burglars occasionally were unable to gauge the black-market value of their merchandise, especially where they had not dealt with similar property in the past. This could get them into trouble in negotiations with professional fences who, by the nature of their business, were likely to have a better sense of what the property was worth (Klockars, 1974). One member of our sample described being threatened by a fence when, in ignorance of their retail price, he complained about being paid too little for some cabinets stolen during a commercial burglary.

> Well, one guy [that I used as a fence] was a Mafia guy; he switched cars like people switch socks. I didn't even know his name. He carried a pistol. We got into it one night about some stuff that I had stole from [a local discount hardware store], some cabinets that I had stole. I tried to value them at fifty dollars apiece. I had about eighty of 'em. He only paid me like three hundred dollars and I had to pay the [truck rental] and pay two guys to do it [with me]! So I bitched at him and one night he picked me up and took me to [another discount hardware store] which is right off of Page [Avenue] and I seen the price of forty-nine ninety-five and I was tryin' to get fifty! I thought they were worth more. So he took me down an alley, but it really didn't even faze me; it didn't even scare me really . . . But when that guy put a gun to my head . . . (No. 099)

Despite such conflicts, which perhaps were inevitable given the diametrically opposed economic interests of the parties, it was unusual for the burglars to express strong resentment toward fences. Most of them, seeming to appreciate that fences had to make a living too, tried to adopt a business-like stance of their own in negotiations. The predominant view among them was summed up by an offender who commented: "If you can get a little more [money] out of [the property], fine. Just give me what I ask for it."

The offenders we interviewed realized that negotiation was useless unless their fences were anxious to acquire what they had to sell. Most of them simply relied on word of mouth, common sense, or past experience to determine what items were popular with fences; all were aware that stolen jewelry, electronic goods, and firearms were hot in more than one sense. One burglar, however, was able to go directly to his fences to get a complete inventory of the sorts of merchandise they wanted.

You got to know what to get and who wants it. Most of the
time your fences will tell you what to get. They will tell you
what they are in the market for, you should get this and that.
Plus you know all the other [standard] stuff to bring them.
So therefore you gotta whole bunch of shit to look out for. I
know all kinds of different things to get and sell. I can get
into an *empty* house and come out with five hundred to a
thousand dollars worth of stuff and sell it the same day.
(No. 077)

This offender seldom had to negotiate with any of his fences;
over time the price to be paid for various items had become
established and was understood clearly by both parties to the
transaction (see Klockars, 1974).

In summary, only a minority of the residential burglars in
our sample regularly sold the property they stole to a professional fence. That is not to suggest, however, that such a buyer
was not much sought after by the offenders. Given the opportunity, many (if not most) of them probably would have taken
their booty to a fence. Fences represented a desirable outlet
because they could purchase large amounts of merchandise,
asked few questions, and were motivated to be discreet about
their business dealings. In this sense, ready access to a fence
might have served to facilitate the decision to commit a residential burglary, at least for some offenders, in that the difficulties and risks inherent in locating a buyer did not have to
be confronted. They already had one lined up.

The Pawnshop

For offenders without connections to the world of professional fencing, pawnshops would seem to represent an obvious
alternative outlet for their stolen property. Pawnbrokers offer
customers immediate cash payments in exchange for personal
property on either a loan or purchase basis and thereby provide
a service closely akin to that of fences. And because they
openly advertise their desire to acquire merchandise, pawn-

brokers are easy for offenders to locate. However, disposing of stolen goods through pawnshops is not without drawbacks. The high visibility of pawnbrokers makes them especially vulnerable to police scrutiny; to protect themselves, many require proper identification and will photograph customers before accepting property. In addition, pawnbrokers are notoriously tightfisted with their money, offering only a small percentage of the actual value of the goods being pawned. Many of the burglars in our sample avoided pawnshops for these reasons.

No, [you] can't go [to a pawnshop]; they take your picture in there. And see, the pawnshop have a hot sheet, you know. (No. 006)

[I don't take anything to pawnshops] because the pawnshops won't give me what I want for it. (No. 024)

[I don't take stolen goods to a pawnshop because] a pawnshop wouldn't give you as much of the value of the item. They probably give you fifty bucks [for everything] but [elsewhere] you could get a hundred dollars for each item. (No. 014)

[I avoid pawnshops] simply because if you take [a hot item] to the pawnshop there might be some way [the police] could trace it. Because you got to use your identification on anything that you pawn. So I try and stay ahead of the steps right there. (No. 032)

But 13 of the 90 offenders who addressed the issue of selling stolen goods said that they usually *did* take their booty to pawnshops. Why were they not dissuaded from doing so by the same factors that prevented the other burglars from making use of such outlets?

Most of the subjects who regularly used pawnshops claimed to have a relationship of trust with one particular local pawnbroker (the same name came up time and again) such that they were allowed to pawn stolen property "off camera," that is, without having their picture taken. According to these subjects, the pawnbroker would not accept property off camera from just anyone. However, he was prepared to respect their own desire for anonymity because over time they had proven themselves to be reliable suppliers; they brought him quality merchandise without bringing additional police pressure to bear on his business.

> Well, [this particular pawnbroker] knows me and his workers know me too. So I bring it in and he knows that I ain't gon snitch on him. Usually I try to bring in top quality stuff. That's basically what he's lookin' for. That's how he makes his profit; buyin' good stuff, you know. And after a while you become buddies and he helps you out. (No. 010)

> Well, he's the man. I mean you got certain pawnbrokers who's gonna take you to the third degree — "You got ID?" — and all that. But [this particular pawnbroker] is the man. You go in there and dump [the stolen property] and let him take care of you. I took [him] so much jewelry that, if I'm broke, I can go into [his shop] and get two or three hundred dollars and he could just write me up a pawn ticket; I haven't pawned him nothin'! "[X], I need some money." He'll give me two hundred and give me a pawn ticket cause he know I'm a come back and bring him [some quality merchandise]. (No. 064)

The offenders speculated that this pawnbroker knew full well that the goods they brought him were hot, even though he never broached the subject with them. One burglar attributed this to the pawnbroker's reluctance to confront guilty knowledge, saying, "It's like he's afraid to ask." Perhaps there was a further reason that the pawnbroker did not ask these customers about the origin of their goods; to do so would violate the "norm of silence" that surrounds the exchange of any sort of tarnished property (Shover, 1975:485). As Shover (1975) has pointed out, all illicit transactions are fraught with anxiety and can easily be disrupted by careless talk. Veterans of such

transactions recognize this and keep conversation to a minimum in order to facilitate the consummation of their deals.

Not even dishonest pawnbrokers were willing to accept
items off camera that could easily be traced by the police.
Therefore, the offenders did not typically go to them with electronic goods or firearms because such products carry factory-
stamped identification numbers.

> Pawnshops, they done got strict; they started checkin' serial
> numbers, specially on VCRs. Cause see what the police do
> once a month, they take a list of hot merchandise to all the
> pawnshops within the City of St. Louis and they have serial
> numbers on them. So you don't deal with no pawnshop, pe-
> riod! Unless it's a ring or watch that might be worth some-
> thin' cause it's valuable and it ain't got no serial number on
> it. But like TVs and handguns and rifles and microwaves,
> you don't take none of that stuff to no pawnshop. (No. 046)

They reported that an agreement to transact business off camera was reached most readily in cases where one was seeking
to pawn jewelry because it could be altered without substantially lowering its value; gems could be removed and reset,
while precious metals could be melted down and recast. Moreover, the offenders argued, all pawnbrokers were anxious to
deal with jewelry because they generally knew more about it
than their customers did and thus had a decided advantage in
payment negotiations.

> Oh, you'll get more money off of jewelry than anything.
> You'll never know what it's worth unless you go take it to
> the pawnshop and say, "Well, what can I get for this?"
> [They'll say,] "How much do you feel it's worth?" . . . They
> buy jewelry before any kind of other item because they spe-
> cialize in knowing what it's worth and how many carats it
> has in it. They might tell you it's worth this, but it might be
> worth more. (No. 059)

Some pawnbrokers, of course, would not conduct business
with the offenders off camera under any circumstances. Sev-

eral of the burglars, for instance, told us about a former police officer turned pawnbroker who insisted that all transactions in his shop must be conducted strictly aboveboard. Customers had to provide proper identification and have their picture taken before pawning anything. (We were able to confirm that the pawnshop named by these offenders was owned by an ex-police officer through our informal contacts with the St. Louis Metropolitan Police Department; apparently the shop has become a popular police "hangout" where off-duty officers congregate to drink coffee and socialize.) Nevertheless, a few of the offenders occasionally disposed of their stolen merchandise through strictly law-abiding pawnshops. Some of them paid someone else to pawn the property on their behalf, thereby reducing the risk of being linked to the crime.

> You could walk down the street and get a friend and you say, "Hey man, go in there and see what you can get off of this." They happy, all they want is a few dollars. (No. 051)

> Well, I let other people take [stolen merchandise] to the pawnshop cause I ain't gon put it in my name for it to come back and say I got it. So you pay ten or fifteen dollars to have it pawned for you cause if it comes back, it's gon come on the person who pawned it. (No. 060)

Others simply pawned the property themselves, allowing the transaction to be conducted on camera. Asked whether there was any risk involved in doing so, one such offender replied, "Yeah, it is quite risky, but you figure you'll go on and take your chances." As during earlier phases of the burglary process, these offenders perceived themselves to be in a situation of immediate need and consequently under pressure to act as quickly as possible. No doubt this accounts for their ability to discount the long-term risk of being identified by the police in favor of achieving a short-term solution to their current crisis.

In negotiating with pawnbrokers over the value of property, the offenders adopted a realistic approach. They recognized that such dealers would try to keep their costs as low as possible, and never would offer more than a tiny fraction of the property's market price. Accordingly, they resigned themselves to a strategy that involved trying to squeeze just a little bit more cash out of their transactions. Pawnbrokers offer more money where property is being sold outright as opposed to being put up as collateral for a loan. Most of the offenders, therefore, preferred to sell rather than pawn their stolen merchandise. Even so, they typically made a ritual protest at the pawnbroker's first offer, hoping that it would be increased. Sometimes this tactic was successful.

> [Pawnbrokers] ask you now if you pawnin' this or sellin' this. You tell them you sellin' it. You ain't gon sign shit. [They] put [a piece of jewelry] on the scale and tell you what it is. They say, "Well, I give you a hundred and fifty dollars for it?" "Nah man, you know it's worth more than that!" "O.K., I'll give you two hundred." That's it. Got your money and bust a move. (No. 035)

Because the offenders typically were in a state of financial desperation, however, pawnbrokers almost always had the upper hand in negotiations; they frequently pressed their advantage by refusing to haggle over prices. In effect, they made the offenders an offer and told them to take it or leave it. More often than not, they took it. As one of the burglars explained: "When there's cash in front of your face, it's hard to walk away."

A couple of the offenders usually elected to pawn their stolen property, accepting the reduced payout, instead of selling it outright for more money. One of them said he did so because this actually allowed him to increase his profits. After pawning the property he stole, this burglar peddled the resulting pawn ticket on the streetcorner, effectively getting paid twice for the same merchandise.

> You can call the pawnshop, call them and tell them what you got . . . They gon ask you to bring it in and you bring it in and say, "That's worth such and such a price." They give you a pawn ticket and you take the pawn ticket and put it

in your pocket and go on about your business. Then if somebody lookin' for a VCR or somethin' like that, give them the pawn ticket. You know what I'm sayin'? Just tell them to give me about a hundred dollars and they can [pay to] get it out . . . Like I took this little bitty ol' TV in [to the pawnshop] and they gave me a hundred dollars. So [someone I knew] was lookin' for a little TV. I told him I got one. He said, "Where is it at?" I said, "In the pawnshop." "What you askin' for it?" I say, "Give me a hundred dollars for this pawn ticket." I say, "Here, now you got to get it out." He say, "How much it cost to get it out?" "A hundred dollars." So in one day I made two hundred dollars. That's how you double your money. You know, you take it somewhere else and you sell it for more than what you bargained for, cause I'm a businessman. (No. 047)

The other offender who often pawned goods rather than selling them dealt almost exclusively with gold jewelry. He claimed that he liked to wear such jewelry himself and thus pawned it in the hope that a "big score" would provide him with the wherewithal to buy it back.

[I] just take a loan in case I hustle and make some more money because I like to wear jewelry myself. So I take a loan on it. That way I get about ten dollars. If I sell it, I might get about twenty-five dollars. If you sell it outright, you can't come back and get the shit. But if you get a loan on it, you might make a big hustle tonight: "I got a thousand dollars, I'm gonna buy me an outfit, I'm goin' to the pawnshop and get this jewelry that I ripped off yesterday and I'm gonna be clean." (No. 079)

In eschewing the opportunity to make more money by selling his stolen merchandise on the off chance that he would manage to commit a highly lucrative burglary in the future and be able to retrieve it, this subject was displaying the hopeless optimism that characterized the behavior of many of our offenders. Much of their day-to-day lives seemed to be predicated on the belief that the answer to all of their problems was no further away than the next break-in.

In brief, some offenders without good connections to professional fences saw pawnshops as reasonable alternative outlets for their stolen property. Dealing with pawnshops, however, could be risky; as legal establishments subject to regular police scrutiny, they have a stake in protecting their image of legitimacy. Worse yet for burglars, they are supposed to keep an official record of their transactions, complete with a photograph of each customer, specifically for the purpose of discouraging the pawning of hot merchandise. Most of the offenders who used pawnshops did so only because they had managed to reach an agreement with one particular pawnbroker whereby their transactions could be conducted off camera. These subjects were given special consideration because they regularly had brought in high-quality property without attracting the attention of the police. Not all offenders, of course, possessed the necessary interpersonal skills to negotiate such an agreement in the first place. Those who lacked such skills were left with the option of pawning their booty on camera — and taking their chances — or finding another way of converting it into cash.

The Drug Dealer

Many of the tough inner-city neighborhoods of St. Louis have an informal economy that operates in part on the sale of stolen property. Local drug dealers often play a prominent role in this economy, both as buyers and as sellers, because they have access to ready cash and good illicit connections to potential customers. Twenty-one of the burglars in our sample (23 percent of those we spoke to about the issue) said they routinely took advantage of this fact by selling the items they stole to the neighborhood "dope man."

Sell [my stolen property] to dope men, big dope men, sell it
on the streets . . . That's the quickest way to get some
money from it. (No. 066)

There's about three or four different people that if they
won't take it then one of their friends will. They're people
that make good money; you know, some of them are drug
dealers and they got cash. (Lee Sykes – No. 004)

It be mostly people that you know that probably be dealing
in drugs [to whom you sell hot items]. Somebody that got
the money to buy all the stuff right off your hands. (No. 026)

Basically [I take my stolen merchandise] to dope dealers because they will buy right quick. (John Boe – No. 088)

As noted in chapter 2, getting and using drugs were major
preoccupations for a majority of the offenders in our sample.
Many claimed that they committed residential burglaries for
the sole purpose of supporting their drug use. It is hardly surprising that some of these offenders elected to take their stolen
goods directly to a local dope seller; doing so enabled them to
obtain drugs without first having to convert the goods to cash.
This was an important consideration, especially for subjects
who were intent upon resuming their partying as quickly as
possible.

Most of the time I want to buy drugs, so I take the stuff to
the drug man. Instead of giving me money – he don't want
to give out money cause he's makin' money – so he'll trade
you the merchandise for his merchandise. Color TV, uh, say
about twenty or twenty-one inch might run you three or
four hundred dollars [retail], I'm a give it to him for a hundred and twenty-five dollars. Just trade it and get me a sixteenth [of crack cocaine] for it; a sixteenth will run you a
hundred and twenty-five dollars. That's what I'm gonna do
with the money anyway is buy drugs. So I might as well
check with the drug man first to make a trade . . . nine times
out of ten he takes it all. (No. 009)

Well it depends, you do some [cocaine] before and then want more and have to go and do a burglary . . . [Afterward] sometimes we can take [the stolen property] to the dealer's house and trade it for drugs. (No. 094)

Moreover, taking hot merchandise to a dope dealer was not only a quick way of obtaining drugs, it was also very safe. As one burglar pointed out, "I know [dope dealers] ain't going to want to have [property] traced back cause they selling drugs!"

Like professional fences and pawnbrokers, however, drug dealers often drove a hard bargain in negotiations, offering offenders less in drugs than they felt their stolen property was worth.

Yeah, well, usually there is [a lot of negotiation]. You have to argue with the guy cause they always want to get [your property] for as little as possible so they can get they overhead out of that. (No. 084)

For this reason, several members of our sample who offended specifically because they wanted drugs nevertheless refused to take their booty to dope dealers. They preferred to sell the merchandise elsewhere for cash, believing that having money in hand put them in a better negotiating position with such dealers.

I never take no merchandise [to a drug dealer], I sell that on the street; I get more on the street. If I take it to a bootlegger or somebody that sells dope, they gonna give me what *they* want to give me. They know that I want some shit that bad. I'd rather go sell my [property] to somebody personally and then go back to the dope person with cash money. Then I can start talking deals. It's the way to use your edge, you know, as far as buying shit from the motherfuckers. Excuse my French. (No. 079)

Many of the offenders who wanted drugs, though, continued to approach dope dealers with their stolen property despite an awareness that doing so was not financially efficient. At least in part this can be explained by the perceived pressures of their current circumstances. Simply put, these offenders were in a hurry to get drugs and thus were disinclined to make the extra effort required to maximize their rewards. As several of them reminded us, the merchandise did not cost them anything to begin with; *whatever* they got for it was pure profit. And when that was gone, they could always commit another break-in.

It would be difficult to overstate the disruptive influence of illicit drugs on the market for stolen goods. In neighborhoods characterized by the widespread use of crack cocaine, heroin, and phencyclidine (PCP), addicts have flooded the informal economy with guns, jewelry, and consumer electronic goods. Many of these items have been traded for drugs by their legitimate owners, but many others were stolen and then used for the same purpose. As a result, the price commanded by hot merchandise has tumbled. It is ironic that many of the drug-using burglars in our sample complained bitterly about this state of affairs; they were largely responsible for it!

Friends, Acquaintances, Relatives

In cases such as those outlined above, offenders dispose of their stolen property by selling it at a bargain rate to intermediaries who plan to make a profit by reselling the merchandise. The major drawback for offenders using this system is obvious; intermediaries are motivated to pay as little as possible for the property in order to maximize their own profits. Recognizing this, some offenders attempt to get a better price by selling their merchandise directly to consumers. But this strategy calls for considerable caution; as already mentioned, offering to sell hot merchandise to the wrong person can get offenders into serious trouble. One way for them to handle this problem is to restrict their business dealings to known and trusted customers. That was the solution adopted by 24 of the 90 burglars in our sample who spoke to the issue of disposing of stolen property; these subjects typically sold their booty only to friends, acquaintances, or relatives.

Uh, mostly they be people that I know [who buy my stolen
property]. People that I know like family, or don't have a
whole lot of money and lookin' for a bargain. I know I can
go to a friend's mother and tell them I got a nineteen-inch
color TV and I want seventy-five dollars for it and they jump
on it . . . [E]verybody's lookin' for a bargain and I know if I
go and sell this three-hundred-dollar TV for seventy-five dollars . . . they gon jump on this. Cause everybody's lookin' for
a bargain. (No. 013)

[I only sell to people I know because] you just can't walk up
to anybody and ask them, "Would you be interested in a
microwave oven?" (No. 014)

Well, let's just say [I sell what I steal] to friends. Cause if I
sell it to anybody else, well, who else am I gonna sell it to?
I mean I can't sell it to anybody else off the street cause
that's basically just publicizing me. Why would a man be
selling a gold chain that's worth four hundred dollars in the
store and he sellin' it for about a hundred and fifty or something like that? Why would I be doing that? So I don't trust.
So let's just say it's a matter of trust. (No. 049)

If you deal with a lot of people, then you know a lot of people. Then, basically, some items that you have, you know
these people ain't got. So you could trust these people to the
point that if they got caught, then they wouldn't turn you
in. They'd just say that they bought it from somebody they
didn't know. That's how [other burglars] basically do it and,
as far as that goes, that's basically how I sell [my hot mer-
chandise]. (No. 033)

The fact that these offenders committed residential burglaries typically was well known to their customers. This re-
lieved them of the need to concoct an explanation to make
it appear they had acquired their merchandise legitimately;
everybody knew it was stolen. Often the offenders were approached by a relative or friend with a request for a specific

item. A few of them responded to such requests by making a deliberate attempt to locate and steal that item.

> You know, it's not like I break in this house, [steal the property] and say, "Oh Mack, do you want to buy this?" No! They come to me and say, "I need a VCR." And they are going to pay for some part of my time. Do that make sense? It makes sense to me. It's like you take your car to the auto shop, you got to pay the labor. So that's what that's about. (No. 036)

> What I do, before I even go do the burglary, like I need the money to pay my rent now, then I would have already gotten an order to [get something]. Then this lady [who ordered it] get paid tomorrow, so I got to do this thing tonight. Go out here and get this VCR. And then tomorrow I give it to her. Then I get my money. (No. 044)

The advantage in taking specific requests was that the offenders had a sure customer for their merchandise; they knew that it could be disposed of quickly and profitably. This held special attraction for those who perceived themselves as being in desperate financial straits.

> Well, [I like stealing to order] cause it's less time; it's not time consuming to me. It don't take nothing but five minutes or two or three minutes just to get something and give it to this person . . . They know that you will be there at a certain time, just get it for them . . . and there's your money and you gone out the door. And it don't take no time to do it. (No. 040)

But stealing to order was not always possible on the spur of the moment. Unless requested items were to be found in virtually every residence, offenders often had no reliable way of quickly locating them.

Most of the offenders did not steal goods requested by their friends or relatives "on demand," that is, they did not commit a residential burglary specially to get those items. Rather, they

kept their eyes open for the desired articles during the normal
course of offending, knowing that there were ready buyers for
these things.

> Seem like I know a lot of people. They be tellin' me what
> they want and then they know me [and what I am up to]
> also. Like if I get the stuff, it might be something they need.
> And I just go by there once I get it and bring it to them. They
> have my money right off the top. (No. 052)

Such an approach fits neatly with what we already have
learned about the lifestyle of the majority of these offenders.
Recall that they lived largely for the present moment, with
virtually no regard for the future; as long as there was sufficient money in their pockets, they did exactly as they pleased.
Typically this meant hanging out on the streetcorner with
their cronies, drinking, using drugs, and otherwise having a
good time. Stealing on demand could disrupt this lifestyle because it required the offenders to orient their activities differently, sacrificing their immediate desires to those of their
potential buyers. Few of them would tolerate this disruption,
preferring instead to meet the demands of would-be customers
when and if the opportunity presented itself during the natural
course of events.

One of the most striking things about the offenders who
disposed of their stolen property by selling it to friends, acquaintances, or relatives was that they displayed little inclination to give such customers any kind of discount on the price.
There was almost no talk among them about the need to "help
out" those they were close to. One offender did report occasionally giving a discount to customers she knew to be in serious financial difficulties.

> Sometimes [I accept less than a third of the retail value for
> merchandise] if it's somebody I know. Say it's a poor person
> that want something. They got it! Especially if they got a
> kid and they want a TV to go in the kid's room. They got it!

What the hell am I gonna do with it? I can't set on it. (No. 036)

Even this offender, however, maintained that customers who could afford to pay the going rate had to do so, friend or kinship notwithstanding.

But those that can afford to pay for it has got to give it up. Like I say, if they put a special order in for it, sure they're going to give me a third for it. (No. 036)

When the offenders were under financial pressure and attempting to relieve that pressure as quickly as possible, feelings of loyalty and generosity toward others in their social circle often dissipated rapidly; friends, acquaintances, and relatives came to represent little beyond a potential solution to their present crisis.

Selling to Strangers

While almost all residential burglars would probably pay lip service to the wisdom of knowing those to whom stolen goods are sold, some seldom conduct their business affairs accordingly. Twelve of the 90 offenders in our sample who talked about the disposal of hot property said they usually sold at least part of it to strangers.

Just go in and say, you might walk into a lounge, store or anywhere and say, "I got a color TV or this and that." "And how much do you want for it?" "Blah, blah, blah." "Can I see it?" I say, "I'll bring it to you." (No. 045)

You can go up to a person that is, say, thirty-five and say, "Look, I got a TV, VCR, and stereo. I got an entertainment center. I'll let it go for a hundred and fifty dollars. I'll bring it to your front door. You don't have to let me in or nothing. If you're good with wires, that's cool. If not, I'll hook it up for you, no problem." I sold more entertainment centers that way than Carter's got liver pills. (No. 102)

Man, just like if I see you on the street I walk up and say,
"Hey, you want a brand new nineteen-inch color TV?" . . .
You say, "Yeah," and give me seventy-five dollars. I'll plug
it up for you. (No. 022)

Undoubtedly part of the reason that these offenders routinely
dealt with strangers was that they lacked a better means of
disposing of stolen merchandise. But some of them also
claimed to enjoy the freedom of not being tied to a known
and regular buyer. This permitted them to negotiate each deal
independently of others, without having to worry about putting future business or personal relationships in jeopardy.

They call me the little wholesaler . . . I got my own black-
market scheme. I don't need nobody to help me make my
money. (No. 022)

Although they believed that dealing with unknown customers
was risky, most of them simply accepted that fact, adopting a
fatalistic outlook. As one said: "Walkin' the streets is risky
[too]. Gettin' up out your bed in the morning is risky. You
know, life itself is takin' a chance."

This is not to suggest that the offenders who attempted to
sell their hot goods to strangers were cavalier about the risks
involved, for almost all of them took steps intended to minimize those risks. Most, for instance, avoided seeking buyers
in the neighborhood from which property was stolen for fear
of approaching someone who knew the legal owner. And in
selecting an alternative area in which to tout for customers,
many of them were quite discriminating; they went to neighborhoods perceived as being inhabited by people disinclined to
report their activities to the police. For the majority of these
offenders, this meant sticking to rundown, socially disorganized areas of the inner city where street prices for hot goods
have been depressed severely through oversupply. One burglar, however, often travelled to a nearby university town to
sell stolen stereos, TVs, and VCRs because, in his words, "college students are too hip to go to the police."

Within neighborhoods deemed to be acceptable, the offenders who sold stolen merchandise directly to strangers had clear ideas about the best places to find potential buyers. Foremost among these places were lounges, bars, and taverns; the patrons of such establishments not only had money in their pockets, they also typically were in a mood to spend it.

> You go into a lounge [with hot property], these people be in there intoxicated and they just got paid and they want somethin' for nothin' . . . Go in there and get rid of your stuff like that. (No. 017)

> [A lounge] that's where the money at. See today [is the day for] welfare, welfare checks, food stamps, [and customers] be out there lookin'. They out there lookin' man, they gettin' high and they spendin' up the money. Hey, that's when you sell. Everybody in [the lounge] is happy cause it's money in there right now. (No. 045)

Gas station forecourts and entrances to liquor stores also were popular spots for locating would-be customers.

> [I sell my stolen merchandise] on the streets . . . I've walked up to people at gas stations and have about six or seven rings. I've sold a lot of stuff at gas stations. (No. 057)

These were the last remaining legitimate businesses in many of the neighborhoods from which our sample was drawn. Consequently, they represented the only local places (other than perhaps drug houses) where the offenders could intercept people who were likely to have some ready cash available.

Most of the offenders did not approach every person they encountered as a potential customer for their stolen merchandise. From their perspective, it was unwise to take the risk of offering to sell such merchandise to those with little interest in purchasing it. Accordingly, they made subtle judgments concerning the willingness of each potential consumer to buy the sort of property that made up their current inventory. As one of them explained: "You don't just ask anybody, you got to read your people somewhat." In making these judgments, the offenders often relied heavily on an individual's age.

> People my age and shit, they are more off into stereos. You can occasionally sell a TV to a person in their fifties and sixties, but TVs normally go in the forties [age] group because they are more laid back, wanting to watch TV and shit. But basically the TV, stereo, VCR is all sold within the twenties and thirties group. (No. 102)

Gender also had a strong influence on their assessment of whether a given person represented a possible buyer. The burglar quoted below only occasionally sold hot goods to strangers. However, he provided us with the most complete account of the role of gender in the selection of would-be customers.

> You figure if a person is in a lounge, he's got money to spend. So you just go in there and you see people at the bar and you just about know who to ask and who not to ask. Women, most women are generally off into microwaves and color TVs. So you just start in the back and work your way to the front: "Say, do you want to buy a microwave or this color TV? I got it out here in the ride, want to check it out?" (No. 046)

Beyond these objective characteristics, though, intuition, too, played a part in leading the offenders to approach particular individuals. As one told us: "I don't know why I picks people [to sell stolen goods to]; they be lookin' like they be game to buy somethin'."

Even after the offenders had identified someone as a potential buyer, they continued to make further judgments about that person's attitude toward purchasing stolen property. Some people are unbothered by the fact that merchandise being offered for sale is hot. Indeed, they may regard this as a positive sign, indicating a particularly good bargain (Henry, 1978; Walters, 1985). Other people, however, are strictly opposed to buying anything they know to be stolen. Thus, the offenders attempted to tailor their sales pitch to suit the perceived position of the would-be consumer. Again, the most coherent reference to this practice was made by a subject who only occasionally sold stolen property to strangers.

> I tell [some of] them it's hot. Some of them I tell them it's just mine, I just need some money to buy me somethin'. "This is mine, it's not hot or nothing. I'm selling it to you for this low, low price so I can buy some gas. I need some drugs; it's mine, it's not hot." I could have just stole it from my girlfriend [that] morning. (No. 079)

The above observations might lead one to conclude that the burglars who sold goods to strangers invariably were cautious and deliberate in soliciting potential customers. In reality, however, that was not always the case. Over the course of the study, a number of them offered to sell *us* stolen property, sometimes within minutes of being introduced to us! (Obviously, we declined all such offers, though the project field-worker admitted to us that he occasionally found it difficult to turn down a good deal.) This lack of caution underscores the dearth of viable outlets for disposing of stolen merchandise available to these offenders; they had access to few people with sufficient money on hand to purchase their goods. As financial pressures mounted, therefore, they became increasingly desperate and responded by broadening the scope of their sales strategy to include a wider range of would-be consumers.

Keeping Stolen Property

With the exception of consumables such as alcohol, drugs, and cash, none of the offenders made a habit of keeping the goods they stole. Nevertheless, some of them occasionally kept a portion of their booty for personal use. The items most likely to be retained by the burglars were handguns and jewelry. Guns could be used both for self-protection and for committing other sorts of crimes. Firearms had symbolic appeal as well; carrying a gun enhanced the streetcorner reputation of the offenders as being "ruthless." Similarly, the ostentatious display of expensive jewelry conferred status on the burglars among their peers (Katz, 1988; Shover and Honaker, 1992).

While these items often were highly prized by the offenders, they seldom remained in their possession for very long. As noted in chapter 2, their lives revolved around a street culture that emphasized high-living and enjoyment of the moment to the detriment of even the most basic level of financial security. This meant that the burglars were under intense pressure to obtain some fast cash on an almost daily basis. A quick way of making that cash was to sell anything of value they could lay their hands on. Guns and jewelry, because they were easily sold, often were the first things to go in this process.

Summary

For most of the offenders, a residential burglary was not complete until they had converted the stolen property into cash. They attempted to do this as quickly as possible so as to be able to relieve the financial pressure that typically drove them to offend in the first place. Despite their hurry, however, the offenders had to be careful to avoid offering their merchandise to someone who might make trouble for them by, for example, going to the police. The majority of them tried to minimize this threat by approaching only those they knew to be interested in buying hot property. For many this meant taking their booty to a professional fence, a dishonest pawnbroker, or a drug dealer. Others sold their merchandise to friends, relatives, or acquaintances, often having received a casual request for the property prior to acquiring it. In each of these cases, transactions typically could be conducted in a matter-of-fact manner owing to an established relationship of trust between seller and buyer.

Just a few of the burglars routinely dealt with strangers in disposing of their stolen goods. These offenders also frequently took steps to reduce the risk of approaching the wrong person as a potential buyer. Most sought customers only in locales populated by people who, in their view, were unmotivated to call the police. And even within such areas not every person was treated as a would-be consumer; those who were approached often had been specially selected because they were perceived to be willing to purchase a particular sort of hot merchandise. Judgments about potential buyers were made using both objective criteria (e.g., an individual's approximate age) and intuition. But not all of the offenders were always so discriminating in seeking customers for their stolen property. As the pressure to get rid of that property increased, some of them responded by offering to sell it to virtually everyone they encountered during their daily rounds.

Regardless of the way in which the offenders elected to sell their hot merchandise, they never realized more than a small fraction of its retail value. Thinking only about the necessity of getting enough money to meet a pressing need, most of them did not make the effort required to negotiate the best possible price for their goods; they took what the buyer offered with little or no protest. With this cash in hand, the vast majority of the offenders made haste to resolve whatever crisis had prompted their offense (e.g., paying outstanding bills or traffic tickets or, more likely, buying drugs) so that they could resume the partying that is such a prominent feature of street-life. As discussed in chapter 2, this partying almost certainly leads to the commission of another offense. Jackson noted many years ago that the commitment of property offenders to partying is the engine that powers their lawbreaking:

> [Burglars], if they had any money, . . . wouldn't be out stealing, they'd be partying. It's as simple as that. If they have money, they're partying, and when they're broke, they start stealing again. (Jackson, 1969:136)

In short, the residential burglaries committed by many of the offenders in our sample had a decidedly cyclical character governed by an intense engagement with activities such as drinking and drug taking that were supported by street culture.

Simply put, much of their offending was directed toward obtaining the funds necessary to sustain activities that constituted the essence of streetlife. We will consider the implications of this fact in chapter 7.

7 Residential Burglary: Theory and Prevention

WE BEGAN THIS BOOK with the bold assertion that an understanding of the active offender's perspective on residential burglary was crucial for criminological theory and for crime prevention policy. Five chapters elaborated on that perspective. Now it is time to make good on the premise that our approach is relevant to theory and policy. We set out in the following sections the implications of our work (1) for explanations of criminal decision making and (2) for the prevention of residential break-ins.

Explaining Offender Decision Making

Numerous attempts have been made during the past decade to explain the perceptual processes that property offenders go through when they decide to commit their crimes. Most explanations fall within the ambit of rational choice theory. Rational choice theorists believe that the decision to offend is the outcome of a deliberate weighing, however rudimentary, of potential costs and rewards (Clarke and Cornish, 1985; Coleman and Fararo, 1992; Cornish and Clarke, 1986). This position has relied primarily on "armchair theorizing" (Clarke and Cornish, 1985:166). As a result, decision-making models generally have been skeletal and abstract and have greatly oversimplified a highly complex process (Shover, 1991). This does not mean that rational choice explanations are erroneous. Indeed, several recent qualitative studies of the process of residential burglary have supported the notion that property criminals make conscious choices during the enactment of their offenses (e.g., Bennett and Wright, 1984; Cromwell et al., 1991; Walsh, 1980a).

Rational choice explanations, however, leave many gaps in our understanding of how offenders make their decisions. It is widely accepted, for instance, that whatever rationality is shown by offenders is of a "bounded" or "limited" variety (see, e.g., Walsh, 1986), that is, it does not take into account all of the information theoretically available to them. Why is this so? And what do these boundaries or limitations consist of? Rational choice explanations are poorly suited to answering such questions because they focus on the objective properties of the immediate criminal situation and pay scant attention to the subjective influence of emotions on offender decision making (Scheff, 1992). This is a serious omission. As Shover (1991:103) has argued: "Whereas the model criminal decision-maker [posited by rational choice theorists] is never angry, desperate, or defiant, the moods of real-life decisionmakers can distort the criminal calculus severely and make offenders unconcerned about risk." Even more serious is the failure of rational choice explanations to take account of the wider cultural context within which offenders decide to commit their offenses. Actual decisions are never made in a vacuum; they are embedded in and shaped by an individual's socio-cultural "matrix of evaluation" (Lofland, 1969:48). The potential costs and rewards attached to any course of action will be evaluated with reference to cultural symbols and values.

Katz (1988) has put forward an alternative explanation of decision making, emphasizing the causal importance of emotional forces to the virtual exclusion of utilitarian calculations of the material risks and benefits of offending. Katz argues that a "person's material background will not determine his intent to commit a crime," though it might influence the form that the crime takes (Katz, 1988:315–16). Exploring factors that shape (as opposed to cause) offending, Katz touches on the role of sociocultural conditions in the promotion of different styles of deviance. The thrust of his explanation, however, remains the supremacy of emotional states as criminogenic agents in the decision-making calculus of offenders. Katz's explanation represents an important counterbalance to rational choice interpretations, but his denial that the intention to commit an offense is linked to offenders' assessments of their material circumstances lies uneasily amongst a wealth of criminological research that indicates that the need or desire for money is the primary motivation for most property crimes (e.g., Bennett and Wright, 1984; Cromwell et al., 1991; Rengert and Wasilchick, 1985; Walsh, 1980a). Emotions clearly have a significant influence on the decision making of property criminals, but a more satisfactory explanation must demonstrate how and why mental states are related to the pursuit of material gain so that a crime results. We contend that this cannot be done adequately without examining the part played by cultural forces in motivating the decision to commit an offense.

It is ironic that a far more comprehensive interpretation of offender decision making than those provided by contemporary theorists has almost been forgotten by criminologists for a quarter of a century (but see Hepburn, 1984). In 1969, John Lofland observed that, at the most general level, the decision to carry out almost any sort of crime was the result of "three sequential and cumulating phases of [the offender's] subjective experience" (p. 41). The process begins, Lofland maintained, with a perceived threat, moves to a state of psychosocial encapsulation wherein the perceived risks of offending become attenuated, and culminates with a specific criminal act. Lofland argued that each phase was independent, in the sense that one did not *necessarily* lead to the next, though noncriminal options increasingly came to be seen as unavailable as individuals progressed through the specified phases. To illustrate this process, Lofland employed the analogy of a leaky funnel:

> The theoretical imagery involved is that of a funnel with numerous holes at the top and fewer holes toward the bottom. As fluid moves through the funnel, there is an enormous initial slippage or loss [resulting from the ready availability of alternative flow paths] but rapidly decreasing loss [owing to a reduction in such alternatives] as the fluid moves downward. (Lofland, 1969:42)

In other words, most perceived threats do not lead to psychosocial encapsulation; but a state of encapsulation enhances the likelihood of a criminal act. The task for criminological researchers, as Lofland (1969:42) saw it, was to identify "elements and states and combinations of elements" that facilitate the movement of individuals through the three-phase sequence leading to crime. What is the nature of the threats that set offender decision making into motion? In what circumstances do these threats lead to encapsulation? And what are the conditions that cause encapsulated individuals to act in a criminal manner?

Lofland attempted to answer these questions by means of a detailed, if speculative, outline of the important cultural, emotional, and physical factors involved in the process. Perceived threats, he observed, can involve either the possibility of physical harm or the risk of social disgrace in the eyes of relevant others. In modern societies, with elaborate law enforcement and social welfare mechanisms, the latter source of threat is the more common. Further, Lofland (1969:48) suggested that certain people are more prone than others to define events as threatening, most notably those "with a weak or attenuated sense of their social worth." Since the genesis of the threats is usually social they can be understood fully only with reference to prevailing sociocultural conditions.

The emotional distress that accompanies a perceived threat, Lofland speculated, is more likely to lead individuals into a state of psychosocial encapsulation when certain conditions prevail. First, the threat must be immediate, allowing little time for reflection regarding the most appropriate course of action. Second, the threat should be experienced infrequently (this is a relative concept), so that it is not well anticipated. Third, the threat must arise in circumstances where the individual is or feels socially isolated, that is, unable or unwilling to get help or to seek advice from others who might intervene to prevent a slide into desperation.

While Lofland (1969:53) observed that encapsulation does not lead inexorably to closure on a criminal act, he nevertheless maintained that it encourages a preference for "simple, short-term, quick and close-at-hand" methods of dealing with the threat. Many of these methods are likely to be illegal. An encapsulated individual will close in on the commission of a crime where the act represents the "most proximate and performable" behavior among the range of realistically available options (Lofland, 1969:61). Situational features associated with the immediate physical environment, especially the availability of suitable targets and tools, often play a role in facilitating the decision to commit an offense. Beyond the physical characteristics of the immediate situation, Lofland also identified everyday routines and social relationships as important crime facilitants. Finally, he argued that individuals may bring certain attributes to the decision-making situation that serve to facilitate a criminal act. These attributes include knowledge and skills conducive to a particular sort of offending and a subjective willingness or openness to the idea of carrying out an offense.

The speculative interpretation of offender decision making offered by Lofland closely parallels the process by which the residential burglars in our sample decided to commit their break-ins. All but a few of the offenders we interviewed typically began to contemplate the commission of their burglaries while under intense emotional pressure to obtain money as quickly as possible. Their sense of financial desperation was created by a perceived threat that they believed could be lessened or removed by the acquisition of cash. The overwhelming majority of them, however, spent much of the money they acquired on high-living (especially illicit drug and alcohol use) and status-enhancing goods. This suggests that the perceived threats had less to do with physical survival than with sociocultural conditions that shaped their day-to-day lives. Bear in mind that these offenders almost invariably were strongly committed to streetlife; many did not have a permanent dwelling or stable social relationships, with the loose, volatile friendships of the streetcorner or front stoop representing their strongest attachments to others (see Miller, 1958). Streetlife revolves around partying, "the enjoyment of 'good times' with minimal concern for obligations and commitments that are external to the . . . immediate social setting" (Shover and Honaker, 1992:285). Participants in the street culture use drugs and drink alcohol literally as if there were no tomorrow. Such activities are cash intensive; sustaining them for any period of time requires considerable resourcefulness. Those with the ability to do so, whether by legal or illegal means, are accorded respect and high status. Participants unable to generate funds necessary to sustain these activities are liable to be labelled "scum bums" and excluded from the action. It is easy to appreciate why many of the offenders we spoke to — addicts and nonaddicts alike — regarded the lack of money to buy drugs and alcohol as an immediate threat to their social standing. To be seen as hip on the street, one must be able to keep the party going.

By no means did the offenders always respond to the pressure to obtain some fast cash for partying by committing an offense. Some borrowed money from a friend or relative. But the fact that most were socially isolated often made this an impractical option. Beyond pragmatic difficulties, some male offenders were dissuaded from asking others for help because they adhered to the masculine ideal of independence and self-reliance that is strongly promoted in street culture (see, e.g., Miller, 1958; Shover and Honaker, 1992). Recall, for example, the offender who told us: "I like to stand on my own two feet as a man . . . and I don't like to ask nobody for nothin' . . . I'm a man, so I take care of myself."

Social isolation and adherence to the masculine ideal of autonomy, then, frequently combined to limit the actual or perceived alternatives open to the offenders for dealing quickly and legally with their immediate need for money. This moved them toward a state of psychosocial encapsulation. Feeling increasingly desperate, the offenders began seriously to contemplate the possibility of committing a crime. The possible negative consequences of offending typically receded into the background as they deliberated how to resolve their financial crisis (see chapter 4).

The decision-making calculus of the offenders also frequently was limited by the spontaneous nature of streetlife. Street culture places great emphasis on the virtues of spontaneity, eschewing "rationality and long-range planning . . . in favor of enjoying the moment" (Shover and Honaker, 1992:283). Offenders seldom anticipated and prepared for the inevitable exhaustion of their supply of drugs and alcohol. When this occurred, it was experienced (against all odds because this was *not* an infrequent event) as a crisis, placing the offenders under the gun to act quickly, lest their street reputation as resourceful hustlers be jeopardized. This facilitated the encapsulation process by focussing their attention on uncomplicated, short-term, and often illegal methods of ameliorating the crisis to the exclusion of solutions that might be more satisfactory in the long run (see, e.g., Lemert, 1953; Lofland, 1969).

Having entered a state of encapsulation, the offenders now were in a position of "more than usual openness to the class of proximate, simple and effective acts which [were] responsive to" their current crisis (Lofland, 1969:60). Virtually all such acts available to them were against the law. But why did they elect to commit a residential burglary instead of some other crime? The short answer, following Lofland, is that the burglary was dictated by a number of objective and subjective conditions that coalesced to make this course of action appear logical. It is in this regard that it becomes significant that a majority of the offenders usually had a specific target lined up and had reasonably good intelligence about that target (e.g., the daily routine of the occupants) before deciding to commit a residential burglary (see chapter 3). Under pressure and desperate for a quick way out of their difficulty, it is natural that they concluded, perhaps almost automatically, that the time was right for exploiting such a situation. Besides, the universe of offense possibilities frequently was restricted by such things as their lack of transportation and the time of the day.

Easy access to the necessary hardware was another feature of the immediate physical environment that facilitated the decision to commit a residential burglary. A typical dwelling can be broken into using nothing more sophisticated than common household tools. This appealed to the offenders, who were anxious to put the offense behind them as soon as possible. Equally important to many of them was the fact that residential burglary did not require a firearm.

The everyday routines associated with streetlife also led offenders toward the commission of a residential burglary. The offenders typically spent many hours "hanging out" with their peers on corners or front stoops. In doing so, they inevitably became familiar with their immediate surroundings: matters such as the comings and goings of neighbors, the delivery of newly purchased goods, and the level of attention paid to household security. When the pressure mounted to acquire fast cash, the knowledge that the offenders had amassed about the local environment frequently crystallized to suggest that a particular residence offered a quick solution to their problem.

The social relationships characteristic of streetlife sometimes facilitated the process of closing on a residential break-in by supplying the offenders with a stock of inside information about promising targets (see chapter 3). In those circumstances, it was not just the availability of a suitable target that prompted the offenders to commit a residential burglary, but also the realization that others expected them to do so (Lofland, 1969). Similar dynamics were at work when the burglars felt obligated to participate in an offense suggested by one or more co-offenders.

The final elements that led to closure on the commission of a residential burglary were the personal attributes that the offenders brought to their decision making. Foremost was their reservoir of technical knowledge necessary to do a burglary. Recent experimental research has shown that, compared to groups consisting of lawabiding citizens, convicted non-property offenders (matched on age, sex, and race), and police crime prevention officers, both juvenile and adult residential burglars have a range of specialized cognitive abilities related to burglary, commonly referred to as expertise (Wright and Logie, 1988; Logie et al., 1992). Such abilities often were displayed by the offenders in our sample. Most had a consistent, workable scheme for assessing risk and reward cues emitted by potential targets (see chapter 3). They also knew numerous ways to gain illicit entry to dwellings (see chapter 4), had a general plan for searching targets quickly and efficiently (see chapter 5), and understood how to convert the goods they stole into cash (see chapter 6). The offenders were not born with these abilities; it is likely that they acquired them through contact with criminally experienced streetcorner peers and co-offenders. Through trial and error they developed a cognitive script that helped them to commit residential break-ins (see chapter 2).

The offenders possessed one further personal attribute that was critical in facilitating closure on residential burglary, namely a moral perspective that made an illegal break-in a "subjectively available" option for responding to their current crisis (Lofland, 1969:84). As noted in chapter 4, most of the burglars said that they experienced little or no guilt while committing their offenses. In the main these were self-centered individuals without strong social bonds; the suffering of others was not prominent among their concerns (see chapter 3). Those few offenders who admitted feelings of guilt were able to carry on with their offenses because their moral qualms were overridden by a desperation to secure some money. They believed that in general it was wrong to commit residential break-ins, but saw themselves as having a situationally justified reason for doing so. That situational justification often involved what Lofland (1969:91) has called a "transcending commitment" to the demands of life on the street. The important role played by subjective availability in encouraging the commission of a residential burglary, however, cannot be appreciated adequately until one realizes that many offenders regarded some forms of criminal behavior (e.g., armed robbery, drug selling) as immoral and thus as subjectively *unavailable* to them. The range of offenses realistically open to the burglars thereby was narrowed, with the likelihood that they would break into a dwelling increasing accordingly.

It was through the cumulative operation of the foregoing objective and subjective conditions that the offenders in our sample came to decide to commit their residential break-ins. These conditions progressively constrained the perceived alternatives open to them while, at the same time, increasingly pushing them toward the commission of a burglary (see Bottoms and Wiles, 1992). It is arguable whether a rational choice explanation of offender decision making can be accommodated within this framework. To do so would require a broad definition of rationality. Such accommodation, however, would not advance substantially our current understanding of the way in which property criminals decide to commit offenses. Though our burglars made conscious choices throughout their crimes (see especially chapters 3–6), their offending did not appear to be an independent, freely chosen event so much as it was part of a general flow of action emanating from and shaped by their involvement with street culture. The highest theoretical dividends, we believe, will accrue from further and deeper research into the link between streetlife and residential burglary (see Hagan and McCarthy, 1992; Shover and Honaker, 1992).

Preventing Residential Burglary

A dramatic reduction in residential burglary rates almost surely cannot be achieved in the absence of fundamental social change. Ideally this change would convince people that it is not seemly to steal the possessions of others. But how to bring about such change is open to question. Standard suggestions for doing so include education, particularly of the moral variety, and the redistribution of wealth (see, e.g., Tunnell, 1992). The assumption is that those who have are less inclined to take what other people have, though the existence of corporate and other forms of white-collar crime offers some challenge to this commonsense wisdom. We would not want to dismiss the potential benefits for crime prevention of large-scale social change, but tactics for accomplishing this are beyond the scope of our present study. Rather, we will restrict our recommendations for preventing residential break-ins to ideas emerging directly from our fieldwork with practicing burglars.

Our explanation of offender decision making paints a portrait of residential burglars who, in the immediate situation of their crimes, perceive themselves as having little choice but to commit a break-in. In broad terms, this suggests two possible strategies for preventing their residential burglaries; we can attempt to keep them from getting into the situation that propels them into burglary in the first place and we can attempt to stop them carrying out the offense successfully.

The first strategy will work only to the extent that it undermines the strong attachment of the offenders to street culture. Much of their offending, after all, grows directly out of an intense desire to participate in and sustain activities promoted by that culture. Weakening the commitment of the offenders to streetlife, however, is a tall order, with formidable obstacles to success. If we take as a starting point what the offenders told us, job creation would seem to be the most promising means of tempting them away from the streetcorner. Many said that they wanted to work and would quit offending if someone gave them a good job. Creating such jobs is a daunting, long-term task. But even if this were accomplished, it is not clear that the offenders actually would be willing or able to take advantage of the new employment opportunities. Not only are the majority of them poorly educated and unskilled, many are unreliable, suffering from drug or alcohol problems, and resistant to following instructions or taking orders. Moreover, by definition, all of the offenders are of questionable trustworthiness. These are not personal attributes highly sought after in a prospective employee. This is not to suggest that expanded employment opportunities will be ineffective in reducing property crime rates in general; only that we are dubious about the impact of a job creation program on the offending of those already heavily involved in streetlife.

There are compelling reasons to suspect that the threat of harsher criminal penalties will not deter the burglars from committing further break-ins. As noted, their decisions to offend almost invariably are made in circumstances where they perceive themselves both as under pressure to act immediately and as having no realistic alternative to burglary. Combine this with the fact that the offenders know from experience that the chance of getting caught for any given offense is small, and it becomes clear why threatened sanctions, no matter how severe, are unlikely to dissuade them from doing more burglaries in the future. Increased penalties for burglary might be successful deterrents only if coupled with detection rates so dramatically improved as to extinguish offenders' perception of the offense as a realistically available option. But it is doubtful that *any* significant improvement in burglary clearance rates can be achieved, let alone an improvement of the magnitude required to act as an effective deterrent.

This leads us to the second broad strategy for preventing residential burglary; stopping already motivated offenders from committing a specific break-in. Here too, however, there are serious difficulties. "Neighborhood Watch," for example, is unlikely to be effective in the socially disorganized areas where many of our offenders carry out their offenses. The residents of such areas often are reluctant to report suspicious behavior to the police, both because they mistrust the authorities and because they fear reprisals from the suspects. Besides, the offenders frequently reside in or near the neighborhoods in which they commit their burglaries; thus their presence is not likely to raise anyone's suspicion in the first place.

That the burglars often offend in their own neighborhoods also undercuts the value of measures designed to create an illusion of occupancy while residents are away from home. Such measures are bound to be less influential where offenders are familiar with occupants' daily routines. And this problem is exacerbated when, as is often the case, the would-be burglars have *inside* knowledge about times when the occupants of intended targets are virtually certain not to be at home. Offenders learn about targets likely to be left unguarded through overhearing conversations at parties, while visiting with neighbors, and by talking with people on the streetcorner. Some find such places while working, or pretending to work, in a job that brings them into contact with local homeowners, many of whom have a careless tendency to let them in on their day-to-day activities. Without wishing to make people unduly suspicious, it nevertheless seems a sensible precaution for them to be circumspect in speaking to strangers or casual acquaintances about their daily schedules. This advice is especially applicable to residents of socially disorganized areas already characterized by high rates of property crime, where there is likely to be a concentration of offenders anxious to acquire such information.

Even when motivated offenders know that a dwelling currently is unoccupied, there remain situational measures that can discourage them from attempting to burglarize it. Foremost among these are occupancy proxies such as dogs or burglar alarms. Few of the offenders in our sample were prepared to tackle these obstacles; most made a concerted effort to avoid them. Another situational measure that can be taken to dissuade burglars from attacking a particular residence involves increasing its surveillability by removing anything that obstructs the view of potential access points from the street and neighboring buildings. Offenders do not want to be seen entering or leaving their targets and therefore show a marked preference for dwellings surrounded by a cover of trees, bushes, or fences.

Where offenders have settled on a specific target, any existing barriers to entry represent the last potential line of defense. Even good, well-installed locks, in and of themselves, seldom offer much protection at this point. That is not because the offenders are adept at picking or breaking them; the majority lack these skills. Rather, it is often simply easier to bypass such devices by breaking a window instead. However, the installation of security bars or storm windows, which are difficult and noisy to break, helps to close off this possibility and thereby makes dwellings less attractive to offenders (see chapter 3).

Once offenders have broken into a residence, strictly speaking the crime can no longer be prevented. But the loss of cash and goods can often be minimized. In chapter 5, we called attention to the cognitive script that offenders use to guide their movement through targets. Typically that script directs them to concentrate their efforts on searching two areas, namely the master bedroom and the living room. Sometimes it includes a quick search of the kitchen and bathroom as well. Offenders are reluctant to deviate from their personal cognitive scripts because doing so can draw them into an ever-expanding search; they might become carried away by the potential reward so that they forget about the steadily increasing risk of detection. Many burglars will not therefore extend their searches to areas such as basements, utility rooms, guest rooms, and children's bedrooms. Valuables kept or hidden in these locations are substantially less likely to be stolen during a break-in.

There is one last issue related to the prevention of residen-

tial burglary that should be addressed: reducing the risk of re-
peat victimization. Throughout our work, we were struck by
the importance that offenders attach to any information that
enhances their ability to make predictions about potential targets. When are these places most likely to be unoccupied?
What sort of goods do they contain? Are they harboring unusual difficulties or risks? In burglarizing a target, offenders
obtain the answers to such questions. Because they know the
site and are aware of what it contains, there are strong incen-
tives for burglars to choose, as a subsequent target, a dwelling
they recently have victimized (see chapter 3). From a prevention standpoint, then, a good time to implement additional
security measures (e.g., the installation of burglar alarms,
storm windows, or security bars) is immediately following a
break-in.

Street-Based Research

The field research for this book was difficult, dangerous, and
expensive. As we trudged with offenders through half-aban-
doned public housing complexes with a bitterly cold wind
howling down the open walkways, it was easy to wonder
whether criminology really needed a study of active residential burglars. After all, a number of researchers already had
explored offender decision making in residential burglary by
interviewing prisoners convicted for such offenses (see, e.g.,
Bennett and Wright, 1984; Rengert and Wasilchick, 1985;
Walsh, 1980a). What more could a street-based study contrib-
ute to our understanding of this process? Now having completed our fieldwork, and with the results of that endeavor in
hand, we are in a position to answer that question.

An initial concern is the distinctiveness of what we discovered through recourse to a street sample. Two of the major
issues we examined – target selection and perceptual deterrence – also have been considered in studies of incarcerated
residential burglars, both in the United States (e.g., Rengert
and Wasilchick, 1985; Tunnell, 1992) and in Great Britain

(e.g., Bennett and Wright, 1984; Walsh, 1980a). This provides a crude baseline measure against which we can judge whether our study of active criminals recruited in a real world setting yielded more and better information. At first glance, things do not look promising; much of what we found in regard to target selection simply parallels the findings of the prison-based projects. While a smaller percentage of the active offenders typically searched for their targets than was true for any of the prison samples, those who *did* search used the same procedures described by the imprisoned burglars interviewed in England and in the United States. Both sets of incarcerated burglars also reported looking for well-covered dwellings that appeared to be affluent and unoccupied (see chapter 3). Likewise, our results concerning perceptual deterrence closely matched those of burglary studies carried out in prisons. In common with Tunnell (1992), who interviewed imprisoned burglars in Tennessee, we found that many offenders handle the threat of criminal sanctions by relegating thoughts about getting caught to the back of their minds during break-ins (see chapter 4). And along with Bennett and Wright (1984), we learned that a number of them used alcohol or drugs to facilitate this process (though, compared to the British burglars, our offenders displayed a much greater tendency toward illicit drug use).

If we look a little more deeply, however, the potential of field-based studies of active criminals to broaden our knowledge of the way in which they make decisions about their crimes becomes evident. Reading descriptions of offender decision making derived from research on incarcerated burglars, one gets the impression that this is a cool, calculating process (see, e.g., Bennett and Wright, 1984; Rengert and Wasilchick, 1985). Our results show that nothing could be further from the truth; the active residential burglars we talked with made hurried, almost haphazard, decisions to offend while in a state of emotional turmoil (see chapter 2). What accounts for these conflicting findings? Cromwell et al. maintain that the difference is due to the tendency of prisoners to reconstruct their offenses.

> We suggest that research reporting that a high percentage of
> burglars make carefully planned, highly rational decisions
> based upon a detailed evaluation of environmental cues may
> be in error. Our findings indicate that burglars interviewed
> in prison . . . , either conciously or unconsciously, may en-
> gage in rational reconstruction—a reinterpretation of past
> behavior through which the actor recasts activities in a
> manner consistent with "what should have been" rather
> than "what was." (Cromwell et al., 1991:42)

Most burglars, whether in prison or not, perceive themselves
as being highly professional in their approach to crime, and
this distorts their perspective on past offenses. As a result,
break-ins are often recalled as though they were committed
in a calm, deliberate manner when, in reality, they emerged
spontaneously in response to the immediate pressures of a particular situation (Cromwell et al., 1991). Such distortion is especially likely with imprisoned offenders. Not only has a
substantial amount of time elapsed since their last free-world
offense in most cases, but there is little or no way of determining the accuracy of their accounts through observation—and
they know it! We are not arguing that prisoners are inveterate
liars but rather that, like all of us, they are anxious to present
themselves as stable, competent individuals; in the calm of
a prison interview room, they are inclined to downplay the
emotional pressures underlying their past offending. The active criminals in our sample, on the other hand, were often
still under the spell of those pressures, and, try though they
might, many were unable to mask the pervasive influence of
these forces on their behavior. Remember, for instance, the
female burglar who told us that she was going to use her interview money to buy a pizza for her children, but then asked to
be dropped off at a crack house instead. Or recall the male
offender who agreed to allow several project consultants to
come along on a visit to the scene of his most recent residen-

tial burglary, only to get incoherently high just prior to our scheduled departure. Incidents such as these represent significant pieces of criminological data because they help to situate the decision making of offenders in the wider context of their day-to-day existence, an existence dominated by the temptations and pressures of life on the street. The prison environment is detached from these temptations and pressures; had our research been conducted in such a setting, we too might have missed the powerful part they play in driving offenders to commit burglary.

None of this should be taken as a criticism of research involving prisoners. Interviews with incarcerated residential burglars have provided a lode of valuable information. Nor can studies of active criminals be justified on the ground that such offenders have special skills and abilities that set them apart from their imprisoned counterparts; we found little evidence of that. Instead, street-based research on criminals is needed because it is the best way to view their offending "realistically," that is, within the larger scheme of their daily lives.

Appendix

Code Number	Alias*	Sex	Race	Age	Age at First Burglary	Burglaries Per Month **	Total Lifetime Burglaries ***	Previous Burglary Arrests	Previous Burglary Convictions
001	Carlion Jackson	M	B	17	16	3–4	9	NO	NA
002	Anton White	M	B	16	14	1	15–20	NO	NA
003	Jayski Jones	M	B	15	14	2	9	NO	NA
004	Lee Sykes	M	B	17	14	1	3	NO	NA
005	Christopher White	M	B	27	18	3	23–25	NO	NA
006	Jeffery Moore	M	B	29	16	5	30	YES	NO
007	Bonnie Williams	F	W	28	18	2–3	300	NO	NA
008	John Black	M	B	24	14	7	650	YES	NO
009	Richard Jackson	M	B	33	15	3–4	40	YES	NO
010	Wild Will	M	B	20	14	1	40–50	NO	NA
011	Jon Monroe	M	B	40	9	3	30–40	YES	NO
012	Bob More	M	B	40	12	1	100	NO	NA
013	Larry Washington	M	B	31	14	3	150	YES	YES
014	Howard Ford	M	B	25	20	2	25	NO	NA
015	Ricky Davis	M	B	34	13	15	60	YES	NO
016	James Cook	M	B	41	21	2	25	NO	NA
017	Larry William	M	B	37	20	5	100	YES	YES
018	Ralph Jones	M	B	36	18	3	20	NO	NA
019	Bobby Brooks	M	B	35	12	4	100	YES	YES
020	Howard Davis	M	B	29	24	8–10	200	YES	NO

	Name								
021	Bob Hill	M	B	30	14	2–3	30	YES	NO
022	Carl Jackson	M	B	30	12	10	350	YES	YES
023	Jade	F	B	30	17	2–3	225	NO	NA
024	Charlie	M	B	35	10	1	200	YES	YES
025	James Brown	M	B	30	14	20	100	NO	NA
026	Tom Bryant	M	B	20	16	1	8–10	NO	NA
027	Diamond Craig	M	B	33	12	2–3	150	NO	NA
028	Mike Bird	M	B	23	15	2–3	100	NO	NA
029	Shannon King	M	B	16	16	1	5–6	NO	NA
030	Mark Smith	M	B	32	18	****	15–20	NO	NA
031	Chris Leisure	M	W	15	13	10	40–50	NO	NA
032	Carl Watson	M	B	26	13	3	30	NO	NO
033	James Wallace	M	B	28	17	1–2	15	YES	YES
034	Genero Ortez	M	W	30	14	1	20	YES	NO
035	Larry Harris	M	B	39	17	2–3	125	YES	NO
036	Running Wolf Woods	F	B	51	19	4	500	YES	NO
037	Larry Williams	M	B	40	20	5–6	100	YES	NO
038	William Jones	M	B	40	17	2–3	100	YES	YES
039	Yolanda Williams	F	B	18	13	4	200	YES	NO
040	Maurice Ross	M	B	33	14	2–3	40–45	YES	NO
041	John Roberts	M	B	38	17	1	110	YES	YES
042	Glenda Harris	F	B	33	15	6–8	130–140	YES	YES
043	Kelvin Perry	M	B	31	17	1	100	NO	NA
044	James West	M	B	24	8	4	50–60	YES	NO
045	Leroy Robison	M	B	38	14	4	250	YES	YES
046	Mike Jackson	M	B	38	17	6–8	900	YES	NO
047	Eric Thompson	M	B	17	6	3	100	YES	YES

Code Number	Alias*	Sex	Race	Age	Age at First Burglary	Burglaries Per Month**	Total Lifetime Burglaries***	Previous Burglary Arrests	Previous Burglary Convictions
048	Billy Kelly	M	B	20	13	10	900	YES	YES
049	Mike West	M	B	18	16	1–2	18–20	NO	NA
050	Bill Anderson	M	B	22	15	****	20	NO	NA
051	John Ross	M	B	33	14	****	1000	YES	YES
052	Larry Brown	M	B	40	22	1	60	YES	YES
053	Tony Smith	M	B	21	15	5	130	YES	NO
054	Jack Daniel	M	B	33	19	2	25	NO	NA
055	Wayne Jones	M	B	31	14	7	1000	YES	YES
056	Joe Outlaw	M	B	40	16	8–12	350	YES	YES
057	Rodney Price	M	B	23	13	1–2	150	YES	NO
058	Roger Brown	M	B	18	13	10	70–80	NO	NA
059	Andre Neal	M	B	19	12	3	275	YES	YES
060	Janet Wilson	F	B	31	29	1–2	15	NO	NA
061	Karen Green	F	B	30	25	1	7–10	YES	NO
062	Nicole	F	B	17	15	2–3	20	NO	NA
063	Robert Young	M	B	32	9	8	150	YES	NO
064	Jerome Little	M	B	33	17	8–10	300	YES	YES
065	Larry Smith	M	B	32	16	2–4	50	YES	YES
066	Bernard Smith	M	B	18	15	****	20–25	NO	NA
067	Robert Johnson	M	B	32	15	3–4	500	YES	NO

	Name	Sex	Race						
068	Marie Spencer	F	B	25	17	13–15	1000	NO	NA
069	Kip Harris	M	B	28	17	5	200	YES	NO
070	Rob Newhouse	M	B	20	16	5	100	YES	NO
071	Sharon Adams	F	B	19	13	6–7	550	NO	NA
072	Matt Detteman	M	W	18	16	1–2	20–30	YES	YES
073	Snake Roberts	M	W	34	16	3	50	YES	NO
074	Joe Bob	M	W	15	13	****	3	YES	YES
075	Waxy Warrior	M	W	16	13	3	10	YES	YES
076	Milo Davis	M	W	16	13	1	20	NO	NA
077	John Doe	M	W	17	14	2	50–60	YES	YES
078	Kenneth Thompson	M	B	21	15	6	35–40	NO	NA
079	Die Leo	M	B	29	14	1	200	NO	NA
080	Eddie Cagen	M	B	32	17	10–15	300	NO	NA
081	Karl Alverez	M	W	16	12	2	25–30	YES	NO
082	Ed Alverez	M	W	15	11	1–2	20–25	YES	NO
083	Earl Martin	M	W	33	18	3–4	200	YES	NO
084	Fast Black	M	B	31	15	1	50–60	YES	NO
085	Tony Scott	M	W	17	12	2	15	NO	NA
086	Jack Steiwert	M	W	19	13	5	20	YES	YES
087	Jhon Do	M	W	18	13	3	18	YES	NO
088	John Boe	M	W	16	12	1–2	50	NO	NA
089	Larry	M	W	26	11	2	20–30	YES	NO
090	Ronald Grey	M	W	19	17	****	10	NO	NA
091	Eddy Smith	M	W	20	10	****	50	YES	NO
092	Tina Smith	F	W	21	17	5–10	85	YES	NO
093	Candy Johnson	F	W	19	14	2	15–17	YES	NO
094	Sasha Williams	F	W	21	17	2	4–5	NO	NA

Appendix

Code Number	Alias*	Sex	Race	Age	Age at First Burglary	Burglaries Per Month **	Total Lifetime Burglaries ***	Previous Burglary Arrests	Previous Burglary Convictions
095	Lynn	F	W	18	17	1	6–7	YES	NO
096	Stacy Bailey	F	W	17	16	1	3	NO	NA
097	Money	M	W	17	10	50	2,500	NO	NA
098	Stacey Jones	F	W	18	17	1	8	NO	NA
099	Joe Wilson	M	W	22	15	2	50–60	YES	YES
100	Darlene White	F	W	19	15	10	50–75	NO	NA
101	Dan Ford	M	W	25	13	10–20	200	YES	NO
102	Dan Whiting	M	W	26	18	2–3	30–40	NO	NA
103	Robert Jones	M	W	16	12	****	20–25	NO	NA
104	Kinlock	M	W	22	9	10	200	YES	YES
105	Tammy Smith	F	W	23	22	2	10	NO	NA

*This alias was chosen by the offender
**This figure represents the average monthly rate of offending over the most recent active period, usually the six months prior to interview
***This figure represents what the offender regarded as a conservative estimate
****Less than one burglary per month

References

Amir, M. (1971), *Patterns in Forcible Rape*, Chicago: University of Chicago Press.

Anderson, E. (1990), *Street Wise: Race, Class, and Change in an Urban Community*, Chicago: University of Chicago Press.

Bennett, T., and Wright, R. (1983), "Offenders' Perception of Targets," *Home Office Research Bulletin* 15:18–20, London: Home Office Research and Planning Unit.

———. (1984), *Burglars on Burglary: Prevention and the Offender*, Aldershot: Gower.

Berk, R., and Adams, J. (1970), "Establishing Rapport with Deviant Groups," *Social Problems* 18:102–17.

Beyleveld, D. (1980), *A Bibliography on General Deterrence Research*, Farnborough: Saxon House.

Biernacki, P., and Waldorf, D. (1981), "Snowball Sampling: Problems and Techniques of Chain Referral Sampling," *Sociological Methods & Research* 10:141–63.

Black, D. (1983), "Crime as Social Control," *American Sociological Review* 48:34–45.

Blumstein, A., and Cohen, J. (1979), "Estimation of Individual Crime Rates from Arrest Records," *Journal of Criminal Law and Criminology* 70:561–85.

Bottoms, A., and Wiles, P. (1992), "Explanations of Crime and Place." In Evans, D., Fyfe, N., and Herbert, D., *Crime, Policing and Place: Essays in Environmental Criminology*, pp. 11–35, London: Routledge.

Bovet, L. (1951), *Psychiatric Aspects of Juvenile Delinquency*, Geneva: World Health Organization.

References

Brantingham, P., and Brantingham, P. (1981), *Environmental Criminology*, Beverly Hills, CA: Sage.

Chambliss, W. (1975), "On the Paucity of Research on Organized Crime: A Reply to Galliher and Cain," *American Sociologist* 10:36–39.

Clarke, R., and Cornish, D. (1985), "Modeling Offenders' Decisions: A Framework for Research and Policy." In Tonry, M., and Morris, N., *Crime and Justice: An Annual Review of Research*, vol. 6, pp. 147–85, Chicago: University of Chicago Press.

Coleman, J., and Fararo, T. (1992), Introduction. In Coleman, J., and Fararo, T., *Rational Choice Theory: Advocacy and Critique*, pp. ix–xxii, Newbury Park, CA: Sage.

Cornish, D., and Clarke, R. (1986), Introduction. In Cornish D., and Clarke, R., *The Reasoning Criminal: Rational Choice Perspectives on Offending*, pp. 1–16, New York: Springer-Verlag.

Cressey, D. (1953), *Other People's Money*, Glencoe, IL: Free Press.

Cromwell, P., Olson, J., and Avary, D. (1991), *Breaking and Entering: An Ethnographic Analysis of Burglary*, Newbury Park, CA: Sage.

Decker, S., Wright, R., Redfern, A., and Smith, D. (1993), "A Woman's Place Is in the Home: Females and Residential Burglary," *Justice Quarterly* 10:143–62.

Dingle, D. (1991), "Ripped Off: As Burglaries Peak This Month, Here's How to Protect Your Home and Family," *Money* 1:96–110.

Dunlap, E., Johnson, B., Sanabria, H., Holliday, E., Lipsey, V., Barnett, M., Hopkins, W., Sobel, I., Randolph, D., and Chin, K. (1990), "Studying Crack Users and Their Criminal Careers: The Scientific and Artistic Aspects of Locating Hard-to-Reach Subjects and Interviewing Them About Sensitive Topics," *Contemporary Drug Problems* 17:121–44.

Feeney, F. (1986), "Robbers as Decision-Makers." In Cornish, D., and Clarke, R., *The Reasoning Criminal: Rational Choice Perspectives on Offending*, pp. 53–71, New York: Springer-Verlag.

Felson, M. (1986), "Linking Criminal Choices: Routine Activities, Informal Control, and Criminal Outcomes." In Cornish, D., and Clarke, R., *The Reasoning Criminal: Rational Choice Perspectives on Offending*, pp. 119–28, New York: Springer-Verlag.

Forgas, J. (1979), *Social Episodes: The Study of Interaction Routines*, London: Academic Press.

Forrester, D., Chatterton, M., and Pease, K. (1988), *The Kirkholt Burglary Prevention Project*, London: Her Majesty's Stationery Office.

Glassner, B., and Carpenter, C. (1985), *The Feasibility of an Ethnographic Study of Property Offenders: A Report Prepared for the National Institute of Justice*, Washington, D.C.: National Institute of Justice. Mimeo.

Gottfredson, M., and Hirschi, T. (1987), "The Positive Tradition." In Gottfredson M., and Hirschi, T., *Positive Criminology*, pp. 9–22, Beverly Hills, CA: Sage.

Hagan, J., and McCarthy, B. (1992), "Streetlife and Delinquency," *British Journal of Sociology* 43:533–61.

Hagedorn, J., (1990), "Back in the Field Again: Gang Research in the Nineties." In Huff, R., *Gangs in America*, pp. 240–59, Newbury Park, CA: Sage.

Henry, S. (1978), *The Hidden Economy: The Context and Control of Borderline Crime*, London: Robertson.

Henshel, R., and Carey, S. (1975), "Deviance, Deterrence, and Knowledge of Sanctions." In Henshel, R., and Silverman, R., *Perception in Criminology*, pp. 54–73, New York: Columbia University Press.

Hepburn, J. (1984), "Occasional Property Crime." In Meier, R., *Major Forms of Crime*, pp. 73–94, Newbury Park, CA: Sage.

Hirschi, T. (1986), "On the Capability of Rational Choice and Social Control Theories of Crime." In Cornish, D., and Clarke, R., *The Reasoning Criminal: Rational Choice Perspectives on Offending*, pp. 105–18, New York: Springer-Verlag.

Ianni, F. (1972), *A Family Business: Kinship and Social Control in Organized Crime*, New York: Russell Sage Foundation.

Irwin, J. (1970), *The Felon*, Englewood Cliffs, NJ: Prentice-Hall.

———. (1972), "Participant Observation of Criminals." In Douglas, J., *Research on Deviance*, pp. 117–37, New York: Free Press.

Jackson, B. (1969), *A Thief's Primer*, New York: Macmillan.

Johnson, B., Natarajan, M., and Sanabria, H. (1993), "Successful Criminal Careers: Towards An Ethnography within the Rational Choice Perspective." In Clarke, R., and Felson, M., *Advances in Criminological Theory*, vol. 5, pp. 201–22, Newark, NJ: Transaction Books.

Katz, J. (1988), *Seductions of Crime: Moral and Sensual Attractions in Doing Evil*, New York: Basic Books.

Kempf, K. (1987), "Specialization and the Criminal Career," *Criminology* 25:399–420.

Kennedy, L., and Baron, S. (1993), "Routine Activities and a Subculture of Violence," *Journal of Research in Crime and Delinquency* 30:88–112.

Klockars, C. (1974), *The Professional Fence*, New York: Macmillan.

Lemert, E. (1953), "An Isolation and Closure Theory of Naive Check Forgery," *Journal of Criminal Law, Criminology, and Police Science* 44:296–307.

Letkemann, P. (1973), *Crime as Work*, Englewood Cliffs, NJ: Prentice-Hall.

Lofland, J. (1969), *Deviance and Identity*, Englewood Cliffs, NJ: Prentice-Hall.

Logie, R., Wright, R., and Decker, S. (1992), "Recognition Memory Performance and Residential Burglary," *Applied Cognitive Psychology* 6, no. 2:109–23.

Maguire, M., and Bennett, T. (1982), *Burglary in a Dwelling: The Offence, the Offender, and the Victim*, London: Heinemann.

Matza, D. (1969), *Becoming Deviant*, Englewood Cliffs, NJ: Prentice-Hall.

Mayhew, P. (1979), "Defensible Space: The Current Status of a Crime Prevention Theory," *The Howard Journal* 81:150–59.

Mayhew, P., Clarke, R., Burrows, J., Hough, M., and Winchester, S. (1979), *Crime in Public View*, London: Her Majesty's Stationery Office.

McCall, G. (1978), *Observing the Law*, New York: Free Press.

References

Merry, S. (1981), *Urban Danger: Life in a Neighborhood of Strangers*, Philadelphia: Temple University Press.

Miller, S. (1952), "The Participant Observer and Over-Rapport," *American Sociological Review* 17:97–99.

Miller, W. (1958), "Lower Class Culture as a Generating Mileau of Gang Delinquency," *Journal of Social Issues* 14, no. 3:5–19.

Murray, C. (1983), "The Physical Environment and Community Control of Crime." In Wilson, J., *Crime and Public Policy*, pp. 107–22, San Francisco: ICS Press.

Nee, C., and Taylor, M. (1988), "Residential Burglary in the Republic of Ireland: A Situational Perspective," *The Howard Journal* 27, no. 2:105–16.

Pettiway, L. (1982), "Mobility of Robbery and Burglary Offenders: Ghetto and Nonghetto Spaces," *Urban Affairs Quarterly* 18, no. 2:255–70.

Polsky, N. (1969), *Hustlers, Beats, and Others*, Garden City, NJ: Anchor.

Rengert, G., and Wasilchick, J. (1985), *Suburban Burglary: A Time and a Place for Everything*, Springfield, IL: Thomas.

———. (1989), *Space, Time and Crime: Ethnographic Insights into Residential Burglary*. Final Report Submitted to the National Institute of Justice, Office of Justice Programs, U.S. Department of Justice.

Reppetto, T. (1974), *Residential Crime*, Cambridge, MA: Ballinger.

Rumgay, J. (1992), *Alcohol, Crime and Judgments of Responsibility: Sentencing Practice in a Magistrates' Court*. Ph.D. Dissertation, London School of Economics.

Scheff, T. (1990), *Microsociology: Discourse, Emotion, and Social Structure*, Chicago: University of Chicago Press.

———. (1992), "Rationality and Emotion: Homage To Norbert Elias." In Coleman, J., and Fararo, T., *Rational Choice Theory: Advocacy and Critique*, pp. 101–19, Newbury Park, CA: Sage.

Sessions, W. (1989), *Crime in the United States*, Washington, D.C.: Government Printing Office.

Shover, N. (1973), "The Social Organization of Burglary," *Social Problems* 20:499–514.

———. (1975), "Tarnished Goods and Services in the Marketplace," *Urban Life and Culture* 3, no. 4:471–88.

———. (1985), *Aging Criminals*, Beverly Hills, CA: Sage.

———. (1991), "Burglary." In Tonry, M., *Crime and Justice: A Review of Research*, vol. 14, pp. 73–113, Chicago: University of Chicago Press.

Shover, N., and Honaker, D. (1990), "The Criminal Calculus of Persistent Property Offenders: A Review of Evidence." Paper presented at the Forty-second Annual Meeting of the American Society of Criminology, Baltimore, November.

———. (1992), "The Socially Bounded Decision Making of Persistent Property Offenders," *Howard Journal of Criminal Justice* 31, no. 4:276–93.

Simon, R. (1975), *Women and Crime*, Lexington, MA: Heath.

Simon, R., and Landis, J. (1991), *The Crimes Women Commit: The Punishments They Receive*, Lexington, MA: Heath.

St. Louis Metropolitan Police Department (1989), *Annual Report—1988/1989*.

Sudman, S. (1976), *Applied Sampling*, New York: Academic Press.

Sutherland, E., and Cressey, D. (1970), *Criminology*, 8th ed., Philadelphia: Lippincott.

Sykes, G., and Matza, D. (1957), "Techniques of Neutralization: A Theory of Delinquency," *American Sociological Review* 22:667–70.

Taylor, L. (1985), *In the Underworld*, London: Unwin.

Taylor, M., and Nee, C. (1988), "The Role of Cues in Simulated Residential Burglary: A Preliminary Investigation," *British Journal of Criminology* 28, no. 3:396–401.

Toch, H. (1987), "Supplementing the Positivistic Perspective." In Gottfredson, M., and Hirschi, T., *Positive Criminology*, pp. 138–53, Beverly Hills, CA: Sage.

Tunnell, K. (1992), *Choosing Crime: The Criminal Calculus of Property Offenders*, Chicago: Nelson/Hall.

Van Maanen, J. (1988), *Tales of the Field: On Writing Ethnography*, Chicago: University of Chicago Press.

References

Vera Institute of Justice (1977), *Felony Arrests: Their Prosecution and Disposition in New York City's Courts*, New York.

Walker, A., and Lidz, C. (1977), "Methodological Notes on the Employment of Indigenous Observers." In Weppner, R., *Street Ethnography*, pp. 103–23, Beverly Hills, CA: Sage.

Walker, N. (1984), Foreword. In Bennett, T., and Wright, R., *Burglars on Burglary: Prevention and the Offender*, pp. viii–ix, Aldershot: Gower.

Waller, I. (1979), "What Reduces Residential Burglary: Action and Research in Seattle and Toronto." Paper presented at the Third International Symposium on Victimology, Muenster.

Walsh, D. (1980a), *Break-ins: Burglary from Private Houses*, London: Constable.

———. (1980b), "Why Do Burglars Crap on the Carpet?," *New Society* 54:10–12.

———. (1986), "Victim Selection Procedures among Economic Criminals: The Rational Choice Perspective." In Cornish, D., and Clarke, R., *The Reasoning Criminal: Rational Choice Perspectives on Offending*, pp. 40–52, New York: Springer-Verlag.

Walters, J. (1985), " 'Taking Care of Business' Updated: A Fresh Look at the Daily Routine of the Heroin User." In Hanson, B., Beschner, G., Walters, J., and Bovelle, E., *Life with Heroin: Voices from the Inner City*, pp. 31–48, Lexington, KY: Lexington Books.

Watters, J., and Biernacki, P. (1989), "Targeted Sampling: Options for the Study of Hidden Populations," *Social Problems* 36:416–30.

West, D., and Farrington, D. (1977), *The Delinquent Way of Life*, London: Heinemann.

West, W. (1980), "Access to Adolescent Deviants and Deviance." In Shaffir, W., Stebbins, R., and Turowitz, A., *Fieldwork Experience: Qualitative Approaches to Social Research*, pp. 31–44, New York: St. Martin's.

Whyte, W. (1981), *Street Corner Society*, Chicago: University of Chicago Press.

Wilson, J., and Abrahamse, A. (1992), "Does Crime Pay?" *Justice Quarterly* 9:359–77.

References

Wilson, W. (1987), *The Truly Disadvantaged: The Inner City, the Underclass, and Public Policy*, Chicago: University of Chicago Press.

Wolfgang, M. (1958), *Patterns in Criminal Homicide*, Philadelphia: University of Pennsylvania Press.

Wright, J., and Rossi, P. (1986), *Armed and Considered Dangerous: A Survey of Felons and their Firearms*, Hawthorne, NY: Aldine de Gruyter.

Wright, R., and Bennett, T. (1990), "Exploring the Offender's Perspective: Observing and Interviewing Criminals." In Kempf, K., *Measurement Issues in Criminology*, pp. 138–51, New York: Springer-Verlag.

Wright, R., and Logie, R. (1988), "How Young House Burglars Choose Targets," *The Howard Journal of Criminal Justice* 27, no. 2:92–104.